# Media and Everyday Life
# in Modern Society

FOR KAREN ATKINSON

# Media and Everyday Life in Modern Society

## Shaun Moores

EDINBURGH UNIVERSITY PRESS

© Shaun Moores, 2000
Edinburgh University Press Ltd
22 George Square, Edinburgh
Reprinted 2003

Transferred to digital print 2006

Typeset in Monotype Apollo
by Koinonia, Bury, and
printed and bound in Great Britain by
CPI Antony Rowe, Eastbourne

A CIP record for this book is available
from the British Library

ISBN-10 0 7486 1179 7 (paperback)
ISBN-13 9 7807 4861 179 9 (paperback)

# Contents

# Acknowledgements

Chapter 2 is an edited and reworked version of 'Broadcasting and Its Audiences', originally published in Hugh Mackay (ed.), *Consumption and Everyday Life*, London: Sage/Open University, pp. 213–46 (© Sage Publications 1997). That material was first written whilst I was employed by the Open University as a consultant author on 'D318 Culture, Media and Identities'. Chapter 3 is an extended and reworked version of '"The Box on the Dresser": Memories of Early Radio and Everyday Life', originally published in *Media, Culture and Society*, Vol. 12, No. 1, pp. 23–40 (© Sage Publications 1988). This research was also discussed in 'Towards an Oral History of Audiences', *Media Education Journal*, No. 5, pp. 50–2, 1986. Chapter 4 draws selectively on material from *Satellite Television and Everyday Life: Articulating Technology* (Acamedia Research Monograph 18), Luton: John Libbey Media/University of Luton Press (© John Libbey Media 1996) – and also from 'Satellite TV as Cultural Sign: Consumption, Embedding and Articulation', *Media, Culture and Society*, Vol. 15, No. 4, pp. 621–39 (© Sage Publications 1993). Chapter 5 is a thoroughly reworked version of 'Television, Geography and "Mobile Privatisation"', originally published in *European Journal of Communication*, Vol. 8, No. 3, pp. 365–79 (© Sage Publications 1993). Chapter 6 draws and expands upon material from 'Media, Modernity and Lived Experience', *Journal of Communication Inquiry*, Vol. 19, No. 1, pp. 5–19 (© Sage Publications/Corwin Press 1995) – and also from 'TV Discourse and "Time-Space Distanciation": On Mediated Interaction in Modern Society', *Time and Society*, Vol. 4, No. 3, pp. 329–44 (© Sage Publications 1995). I am grateful to the publishers of my previous work for their permission to re-use material here in a new form and context.

Another discussion of the data presented in Chapter 7 will appear as 'Identity Remix: Tradition and Translation in the Lives of Young Pakistani Scots', *European Journal of Cultural Studies*, Vol. 2, No. 3, in press. Thanks to Karen Qureshi for agreeing to include this coauthored chapter, which is based on her preliminary research and analysis in an ongoing ethnographic investigation that she is carrying out in Edinburgh. The arguments put forward in Chapter 8 were rehearsed in a paper presented to the 1997 British Sociological Association Conference at the University of York. My initial paper will appear as 'The Mediated "Interaction Order"', in Jeff Hearn and Sasha Roseneil (eds), *Consuming Cultures: Power and Resistance*, Basingstoke: Macmillan/BSA Publications, in press.

Over the lengthy period in which the work contributing to this book was done, I have incurred numerous debts to my teachers, colleagues and friends. In the limited space available to me, it is only possible now to acknowledge a few of these. For the generous advice they gave several years ago – and particularly for the example of their own writings on media and everyday life in modern society – I wish to note the help and guidance of Paddy Scannell, David Morley and Roger Silverstone. My understanding of issues to do with domestic consumption and electronically mediated communication owes much to conversations with Stevi Jackson and Andrew Tolson respectively, and from the outset Mark Hammonds has been willing to talk as we walked, critical of most of the ideas I tried out on him. Hazel Hall and Tim Read also provided good company, distracting me from the wordprocessor at the required times. In addition, I am especially grateful to Jackie Jones at Edinburgh University Press for supporting the current publication. By far my biggest debt, though, is to my partner Karen Atkinson – a past and present colleague – to whom the book is dedicated. I would not have had the confidence to complete the project without her encouragement.

Summer Term 1999

# I Media and Everyday Life in Modern Society

What position have television, radio and other electronic media like telephones and computers come to occupy in people's day-to-day lives and social relationships? How do these communication and information technologies get used and made sense of in local settings such as the household and the urban neighbourhood? How have they helped to construct new arrangements of time, space and place in a culture with globalising tendencies? What types of identity, experience and interaction do the electronic media make available to their different audiences or users? In this book, I offer a particular set of answers to these general questions for media and cultural studies, and the following chapters represent a range of my investigations and reflections on media and everyday life in modern society. In this opening, introductory chapter – which shares its title with that of the book as a whole – I point to some recurrent themes running through my work and situate it within broader developments in the field. I also argue for an interdisciplinary approach to the study of media and modern daily life, in which there is a close connection between theory and empirical research.

## Communication Technologies in Local Settings

My initial interest in this area was developed in the context of an historical investigation into the changing position of early radio in the domestic sphere during the 1920s and 1930s (see Chapter 3). Through an analysis of oral history interviews conducted with elderly people living in a town in the North-West of England, and by drawing on various documentary sources from that period, I was concerned to chart the formation of broadcasting's relationship with household life – a process which the cultural historian Lesley Johnson (1981) has called its 'capturing' of time and space in the home. This involved mapping out the shifting uses and meanings of radio for domestic listeners, both as a technological object and as a provider of programme services – its gradual transformation from being a 'miraculous toy' to becoming an accepted 'part of the furniture'. My research demonstrates that this process had a significant gendered dimension. At the point of its arrival in the home, masculine discourses constituted the radio set primarily as a focus of technical experimentation and adventure. Only later did women start to incorporate the wireless into their day-to-day routines, as changes were made to the form of the listening apparatus and as broadcasters began to address their audience as 'the family' – seeking to construct the cosy pleasures of the hearth.

Although the main aim of this work on early radio was to 'denaturalise' the taken-for-granted place of broadcasting in everyday life – to show how its established presence in the household setting is the outcome of a complex social and historical process – there was another, related aspect of that project which informed my subsequent thinking and research on communication technologies. This had to do with the role of the media in articulating the private and the public, in providing links between the domestic sphere and various 'imagined communities' (Anderson 1983) beyond the local situations of daily living. In the case of radio in Britain during the inter-war years, listeners were offered access to a mediated yet 'knowable' national community which was made available by a system of public service broadcasting (see Cardiff and Scannell 1987). The live coverage of national state or sporting occasions, and the putting together of a common programme schedule targeted at the private family group, enabled listeners at home to make new collective identifications – but as I will discuss at the end of Chapter 3, those identifications cannot be assumed simply from an analysis of broadcast output.

Following that oral history research, which was carried out back in 1985, I came to realise that my own concern with communication technologies in local settings was shared by a number of others working in British media and cultural studies. For example, David Morley (1986) – in his account of TV viewing practices in some London families – looked at the different relations which men and women can have to the television set in the domestic context. Meanwhile, Ann Gray (1987) was interested in how a sample of women in Yorkshire responded to the video recorder – then still a recent arrival in the home. They found, as I did, that the media's uses and meanings for audiences were bound up with issues of gender and power. Their perspective involved situating media consumption within wider patterns of household leisure and labour, and it suggested that there might be fruitful overlaps between reception analysis and a critical sociology of the family (see Jackson and Moores 1995). Indeed, in his later theoretical and empirical work with Roger Silverstone, Morley went on to argue that the study of communication and information technologies must be grounded more fully within an ethnography of domestic cultures (Morley and Silverstone 1990). Referring amongst other things to my investigation of radio and everyday life, these authors also called for further research on the part played by broadcasting in spanning the divide between private and public worlds.

In an attempt to pursue the issues which were being raised by this emerging perspective, I decided to explore another crucial period in broadcasting history. By the late 1980s, policies of 'deregulation' and the marketing of new TV technologies heralded an expanded, multi-channel viewing environment in Britain – and my next research project was to be an ethnographic study of satellite television as an object of consumption, considering important changes in broadcasting culture 'through the eyes' of ordinary viewers who had acquired this technology (see Chapter 4). Between 1990 and 1992, I visited the homes of consumers clustered in different residential areas of a South Wales city – speaking with them about their decision to get a dish, the significance of satellite TV in their daily lives, and their identifications with what Kevin Robins (1989) termed the 'image spaces' of television. Just as Morley, Gray and Silverstone had insisted on locating media use within a network of domestic activities and social relations, so I wanted to see satellite TV in this broader context – plotting its position alongside other communication and information technologies in the home, and understanding the role of its reception in the interpersonal dynamics and politics of households. That meant asking about electronic media such as the computer, the telephone and the hi-fi system – and it demanded that attention be paid to generational divisions as well as those of gender.

Of course, the cultural significance of satellite television in local settings is not limited to the domestic interior, since the dish which is required to pick up transmissions often provides neighbours and passers-by with a visible external sign of possessing the technology. At the time of my ethnographic research, there was some controversy over the siting of these dishes (see Brunsdon 1991). In Chapter 4, I will discuss plural interpretations of the displayed object – its 'multiaccentuality' (Volosinov 1973), to borrow a concept from semiotics – within and across neighbourhoods in this study. Interviewees reported a whole range of emotional dispositions towards the dish, from feelings of pride through to senses of disgust,

embarrassment or plain indifference. I try to relate their responses
to patterns of taste in modern society, identifying the 'distinctions'
(Bourdieu 1984) that are made between classes and class fractions.

When they spoke about the many channels brought to their
screens by satellite TV, respondents often distinguished the American or European feel of programmes from what they perceived to be
the traditional 'Britishness' of terrestrial television – with some
viewers expressing a preference for Sky precisely because it is not
the BBC. If broadcasting in Britain had hailed its audience members
as national subjects, then the 'electronic landscapes' of satellite TV
were more transnational in character (see Morley and Robins 1995).
Programme discourses offered material which viewers could use to
'reimagine' the boundaries of community, although my work was
always concerned to ground such claims in the empirical
complexities of quotidian life. Reluctant to accept the idea that
technology has a direct, straightforward impact on social change, I
was searching for 'interdiscursive' links between broadcast output
and the local circumstances of consumption. In other words, it was
important to find out why certain people identify with new
territories of transmission and others do not.

## Time, Space and Place in Global Culture

Whilst investigating those connections between the private and the
public, I was looking for a theoretical framework which would
enable me to explain transformations in the lives of media consumers – in particular, the shifting arrangements of time, space and
place in modern daily life. To begin with, this led me back to the
concept of 'mobile privatisation' originally put forward by Raymond Williams (1974) in his book on television as technology and
cultural form. I employ that term as my point of departure for a
proposed human geography of TV and its audiences (see Chapter 5).
Then later, I drew on some work by the social theorist Anthony
Giddens (1990) – whose concept of 'time-space distanciation' seemed
to me to be valuable for media and cultural studies. Although
Giddens himself had relatively little to say there on broadcasting or
other electronic media – since he was presenting a wide-ranging and
general account of the conditions of 'late modernity' – his writing
does suggest productive ways of thinking about communication
technologies (see Chapter 6).

Mobile privatisation was the name which Williams gave to a
distinctively modern style of living that is centred on the home yet
based on travel and communication across physical distances,

bringing together two apparently contradictory tendencies in contemporary culture. Critical of a perspective known as 'technological determinism', he nevertheless saw motor transport and broadcasting as key components of this lifestyle. The car allows individuals and family groups to visit places outside the immediate surroundings of their residential area, either for work or for leisure purposes. Similarly, while television and radio have contributed to a domestication of popular entertainment – part of a larger 'withdrawal to interior space' (Donzelot 1980) – they have also opened the household up to electronically mediated public worlds. Broadcasting might be said to facilitate a kind of 'imaginative travel'. As Joshua Meyrowitz (1985) has observed, the walls of the home are now more permeable, and far-away events can be witnessed on TV virtually at the time they happen. This clearly has profound implications for the geography of social activity. In Chapter 5, I will examine television's position within the spatial and temporal organisation of modern society – reviewing relevant literature by geographers, communication theorists and cultural anthropologists.

Chapter 6 is a variation on the same theme, but my starting point here will be provided by Giddens. I have previously made use of his theory of 'structuration' (see Giddens 1984) in an attempt to resolve a debate about creativity and constraint in everyday consumption practices (Moores 1993). In this book, though, my interest lies in his subsequent notes on the institutional and phenomenological dimensions of modernity. He chose to reject fashionable ideas that label the current era a 'postmodern' one, preferring instead to talk of a late modern age in which changes occurring in Europe over the past three centuries have become increasingly radicalised and universalised. Both the pace and scope of change have been dramatic. As the 'juggernaut' of modernity has accelerated, there has been a consequent globalisation of culture – with social relationships getting 'stretched' across broad sections of the earth's surface.

Giddens sought to account for this stretching with reference to a process he called time-space distanciation. In order to grasp that concept, it is necessary to come to terms with his analysis of the transition from pre-modern to modern societies – a break in which time and space were each extended beyond the confines of place, by which he meant situated contexts of co-presence. Whereas 'when' had been associated with a highly localised 'where', time measurement was progressively standardised by the mechanical clock and globalised through the adoption of worldwide time-zoning – and whereas space had tended to coincide almost exclusively with place, it was progressively 'torn' from particular locales. If space still overlaps with place, it is no longer contained there. This is certainly not to say that local settings have ceased to be important in conditions of late modernity – my own research on communication technologies counters such a notion – but it is to recognise that social life has, in many respects, been lifted out of place or 'disembedded'. In these circumstances, there is the potential for new ties to develop between absent others, and for new links to be forged between day-to-day routines and an emerging global culture.

Different types of 'disembedding mechanism' were discussed by Giddens. For instance, he reflected on the role of money as a symbolic token which may facilitate transactions between people who are physically separated – perhaps even on opposite sides of the globe. When it takes the form of information rather than hard currency, like the figures that flicker across international financial markets, money serves to remove business from specific milieux of exchange. It is a means of time-space distanciation. His example is of interest to me because these markets are dependent upon technologies like telephones and computers for their operation, and elsewhere he went on to acknowledge that modernity is inseparable from its media – initially the printed word and then the electronic signal, which brought the possibility of almost instantaneous communication among geographically dispersed populations (Giddens 1991). Along with academics such as Graham Murdock (1993), Roger Silverstone (1994) and John Thompson (1995), I have been concerned to think through the implications of this perspective on modernity for a social theory of the media. In doing so, I have applied a number of ideas borrowed from Giddens – notably his reflections on the disembedding and re-embedding of social systems, on dynamics of trust and risk or senses of familiarity and estrangement, and also on the 'institutional reflexivity' of modern society.

However, my reading of this work – and that of other theorists writing about globalisation and time-space relations – is not uncritical. I believe there has been a tendency in some recent commentaries to overlook the uneven consequences of change for different social groups, coupled with a failure to address patterns of inequality. The globalising of modernity does not have the same universal significance for all the planet's inhabitants, not even for those who live in the relatively affluent 'first world'. Contemporary phrases such as the 'global village' and the 'information super-highway', inspired by increasingly rapid transportation and communication flows, must therefore be treated with caution. Despite the development of international air travel, it is important to remember that everyday life for most people can still involve being stuck in a traffic jam or waiting for a bus which never comes (see Massey 1992). In addition, access to media events and services is ever more dependent upon ability to pay. If broadcasting in Britain was originally intended as a shared public utility, then the trend is now towards subscription channels and pay-per-view transmissions – and whilst a small but growing minority is connected to the Internet via personal computer, it is a sobering thought that the vast majority of the human race still has no private use of a telephone.

### Identity, Experience and Interaction

Throughout the empirical and theoretical work outlined so far – on communication technologies in local settings or on time, space and place in global culture – I have maintained an ongoing concern with issues of identity, experience and interaction. For example, in my research on audiences for satellite TV and early radio, I explored senses of self and community which were constructed from a specific range of symbolic resources available to consumers in their daily lives. These personal and collective identities were both shaped by and shaping social relations of class, gender and generation. They were bound up with regional, national and transnational formations too. Meanwhile, in my writings on media and modernity, the central focus was on how it feels to live in a mediated cultural environment – on day-to-day experiences of mobile privatisation and time-space distanciation. In each of those areas, I was looking at dynamic interactions – either between the co-present consumers of electronic media, or else between absent others who are put in touch by technology. The remaining contents of the book pursue these interests further, beginning with a jointly authored case study and ending with a general analytical essay.

Stuart Hall (1992), in a review of debates about the changing character of identity in modern society, has pointed to the emergence of new ethnicities and 'cultures of hybridity' as a consequence of new articulations between the local and the global. His discussion revolved around a phenomenon which he called the arrival of 'the Rest in the West' – a migration of peoples and signs from Europe's former colonies to its metropolitan centres – and he talked there about the potential this creates for a 'translation' of values and meanings across cultural boundaries. Following in the footsteps of Marie Gillespie (1995), who had investigated everyday translations of that sort by Punjabi Londoners, Karen Qureshi and I have reflected on the lived experiences of some young Pakistani Scots in

Edinburgh (see Chapter 7). Based on preliminary fieldwork which my co-author carried out in 1996, our account charts their routine yet inventive 'negotiations of tradition'. We examine the role of media use in the making of identities – but it is also important for us, just as it was for Gillespie, to understand that activity in a wider social context.

Our metaphor for practices of translation or hybridisation is a kind of music known as 'remix'. Popular among young British Asians, this cultural form combines 'sounds from the East' with a range of electronic rhythms which are drawn from Western youth cultures – so that collision of styles may represent broader patterns of social change within the South Asian diaspora. In Chapter 7, we will try to document the distinctive feel of those shifts as they are experienced in everyday life, although it is necessary to stress that change does not take place at the same rate or in precisely the same way for all Pakistani Scots. Young women and men, for instance, are situated quite differently within this process as they actively fashion their feminine and masculine identities. We aim to describe and interpret the main features of their gendered lives, and to comprehend something of their complex relationships with parents and peers. As well as identifying the creative aspects of media consumption and other cultural activities, our writing attends to the multiple constraints and pressures which are operating in this particular 'diaspora space' (see Brah 1996).

For the young people interviewed in that study, technologies such as broadcasting, telephones or computers were part of the fabric of daily social life – and in the concluding chapter of my book, I offer a wide-ranging discussion of these electronic media which serves to pull together many of my earlier concerns (see Chapter 8). The focus here is provided by the idea that it is possible to speak of a mediated 'interaction order'. Sociologist Erving Goffman (1983) had argued that there was a specific order of human behaviour and social relations which was associated with face-to-face, situated interpersonal contact. In Chapter 8, I will suggest that the same is true of electronically mediated communication. What Thompson (1990) called the 'extended availability' of symbolic forms in space and time has facilitated new sorts of interaction at a distance in modern society – exchanges in which the participants occupy separate physical places, but can nevertheless share an imagined community or 'virtual reality'.

Since the 1970s in media and cultural studies, perhaps the most developed line of work on interactions between the media and their audiences has conceived of that connection as one involving 'texts' and 'readers' (see Moores 1990). This perspective, influenced largely by post-structuralist and Marxist schools of thought, was valuable in raising questions to do with signification and ideology. The researcher might ask, for example, how meaning production and social reproduction – or resistance – are played out in the encoding and decoding of TV discourse (Morley 1980). At the same time, however, those concepts and theories tended to neglect certain basic features of mediated communication – especially what I refer to at the close of my book as its performative and experiential dimensions. In order to come to terms with these things, a different conceptual vocabulary and way of seeing are required. For instance, I have borrowed the notion of a 'para-social relationship' between television performers and domestic viewers from two North American scholars who were writing over forty years ago, Donald Horton and Richard Wohl (1956). They were interested in the apparently familiar, conversational style frequently used by presenters and show hosts to address absent audiences – and in the 'bond of intimacy' which may be formed between them. I am also persuaded by Paddy Scannell (1996), who has insisted recently on the relevance of categories like sociability and sincerity for the analysis of broadcasting. Indeed, it is my contention that those categories are equally relevant to any consideration of communication via the telephone and personal computer, where the distinction between performer and audience is far less fixed and clear.

Having offered an initial definition of mediated interaction which sets it in opposition to situated cultures, I go on to qualify this by emphasising that communication technologies are always knotted into the co-present encounters of everyday life. On occasion, the technological object and its transmitted materials function quite literally as a 'medium' (Lull 1990) – or else what Goffman (1969), from his dramaturgical perspective, would term a 'stage prop' – for localised interactions. In households, neighbourhoods and work or leisure contexts, the electronic media are caught up in interpersonal tactics of 'affiliation' and 'avoidance' – they are used to express feelings of solidarity as well as being a focus of discord. The simple social acts of tuning in, ringing up and logging on can therefore have complex meanings for subjects who are negotiating their relations to immediate others (see Bausinger 1984). In fact, what these practices point to is the way in which situated and mediated worlds constantly overlap in conditions of late modernity. There is a simultaneous mixing of proximate and distant communications.

## Theory, Research and Interdisciplinarity

In preparing the book for publication, my purpose has been not only to compile a volume of writings on media and modern daily life but also to advocate a particular approach for further study. Despite a growing interest in the area during the last few years, there is much more work still to be done – and in a number of the chapters that follow, I make specific proposals which are designed to stimulate new investigations and reflections. At this stage, though, it is appropriate for me to state the general principles of my approach – formed in the context of broader academic developments. These entail a commitment to interdisciplinary inquiry, and to elaborating a theory of the media and modernity that informs and is informed by empirical research on the dynamics of day-to-day living.

The type of research which I favour is qualitative (Moores in press). In contrast to the quantitative methods of 'audience measure-ment' traditionally employed on behalf of the broadcasting industry (see Ang 1991), my preferred techniques for studying everyday media use are conversational interviews and observations of local settings. Ethnographies and oral histories – supplemented by an analysis of public discourses or representations – are well suited to dealing with those issues of identity, experience and interaction that interest me here. They provide raw material for the production of what Clifford Geertz (1973) has called 'thick descriptions' – interpretative accounts of social activity which foreground meaning and emotion. Theory is a key ingredient for this thickening of description. When trying to make sense of what goes on within quotidian culture, I have found it helpful to combine ideas and concepts drawn from various social and cultural theorists – such as Giddens, Goffman, Hall and Williams. In different ways, they have each been concerned with the distinctive character of contemporary existence, and in my view the best of their work has managed to link matters of the self and private life to institutional processes on a national and global scale. Of course, it should be remembered that if theory is to retain its salience and explanatory power, then it must continually be brought into contact with the findings of empirical research. Abstract thought alone often fails to grasp the fine detail of people's daily routines.

Reading back through the opening chapter, I am struck by numer-ous references to the names of academic disciplines and perspectives. There is mention of sociology, history, geography and anthro-pology – as well as politics, semiotics and ethnography – and this gives a clear indication of the book's interdisciplinary nature.

Again, Geertz (1983) has supplied an apt phrase when noting that modern social theory and research are increasingly marked by a crossing of boundaries between bodies of knowledge. He talked about the emergence of 'blurred genres' of inquiry. Stretching his point a little, it could be argued that the field of media and cultural studies is one institutional instance of this blurring or crossing. As a subject in British higher education, it was formed in a rather awkward alliance between academics from across the humanities and social 'sciences' who brought their established knowledges to bear on patterns of communication and culture, yet this collaboration was productive precisely because it enabled them to shed different sorts of light on the problems which they faced. For a 'second generation' in media and cultural studies, myself included, interdisciplinarity comes more easily – although it remains an important goal to strive for in work on the electronic media.

Next, Chapter 2 serves a dual function. It extends discussion of the central themes and issues which have been introduced so far in Chapter 1 – but by focusing on the position of broadcasting as an 'institution in everyday life' (Rath 1985), it also lays a necessary foundation for the detailed analyses of early radio and satellite TV presented in Chapter 3 and Chapter 4. In order to appreciate how audiences for broadcast output were originally constituted, and how they have begun to change over recent years, it is crucial to have an understanding of the ordinariness or taken-for-grantedness of television and radio in the daily lives of most viewers and listeners. Novelty and transformation should be seen against a background of the familiar and the mundane.

# II Broadcasting as an Institution in Everyday Life

Broadcasting may be thought of as an 'institution' in two different senses of the term. On the one hand, it is an industry for the manufacture of symbolic goods. It has various institutional sites of cultural production that are characterised by particular professional practices and by specific relationships to the state or the market. On the other hand, at the point of cultural consumption where those symbolic goods enter into the social settings which are inhabited by its audiences, broadcasting can also be understood as what Claus-Dieter Rath (1985) has called an institution in everyday life – part of the social fabric that goes to make up our routine daily experiences. This chapter will focus on the latter definition – on broadcasting as an institutionalised feature of cultural consumption. However, in looking at the position which television and radio have come to occupy in the day-to-day lives of viewers and listeners, I want to insist that we keep the former definition of broadcasting – as an institution of cultural production – firmly in mind. It is important for us to do so because producers, consumers and the communicative forms which pass between are located on the same integrated 'cultural circuit' (see du Gay et al. 1997).

I begin here by considering the distinctive conditions of production and consumption in this cultural circuit, offering a general account of broadcasting and its audiences to help set the scene. My attention then turns to a critical examination of the industry's own orientation towards its viewing and listening publics, its communicative styles or 'modes of address' and its objectification of 'the audience' as a commodity. I proceed to deal with the significance which broadcasting has in private realms of reception. There, my interest lies in the situated meanings and pleasures that are generated by consumers, and in the social relations of power which operate in routine domestic contexts. Finally, there is an exploration of the roles that TV and radio play in articulating local cultures and globalising processes – putting viewers and listeners in close

listant events, potentially transforming our senses of
...unity. A common theme which runs through this
...rpinning each of these important issues, is broad-
...on within the social arrangements of space and time.

## ...litions of Production and Consumption

...f we are to comprehend the conditions of production and consumption in broadcasting, and the link between those different points on
the cultural circuit, then it is necessary for us to chart their spatial
and temporal dimensions – to identify the dynamics of location and
'mediation' which are in play. Images and sounds get produced and
consumed in places situated at a distance from one another, yet the
moments of transmission and reception in broadcasting are virtually simultaneous. While the place of the studio or outside broadcast is far removed from the dispersed household settings where
viewing and listening are ordinarily done, television and radio
manage to offer their audiences a feeling of 'liveness' and immediacy
– as the organised scheduling of their programmes gets intricately
woven into the rhythms of our everyday lives.

The spatial separation of producer from consumer, combined
with the temporal simultaneity and continuity of transmission and
reception, have given rise to an 'aesthetic' and a communicative
style that is peculiar to broadcasting. Raymond Williams (1974)
made an early attempt to map this aesthetic in his ground-breaking
study of TV. He showed there how the medium's output and the
experience of home viewing are both characterised by what he
referred to as 'the fact of flow'. This was brought to his attention
when, as a regular writer of journalistic pieces, he had tried hard to
develop an appropriate way of reviewing television content – of
finding a subject matter and a method of criticism which were
adequate for the medium:

> Reviewers pick out this play or that feature, this discussion
> programme or that documentary. I reviewed television once a
> month for four years, and I know how much more settling,
> more straightforward, it is to do that … Yet while that kind of
> reviewing can be useful, it is always at some distance from
> what seems to me the central television experience – the fact of
> flow … It is indeed very difficult to say anything about this. It
> would be like trying to describe having read two plays, three
> newspapers, three or four magazines, on the same day that one
> has been to a variety show and a lecture and a football match.

And yet in another way it is not like that at all, for though the items may be various the television experience has in some important ways unified them.

(Williams 1974: 95)

Building on this discussion, John Ellis (1982: 118) questioned the meaning of the word 'items' towards the end of the passage reproduced here, asking if Williams had been wrong to hang on to the idea that flows are made up of independent works or discrete programmes: 'He underestimates the complexity of broadcast TV's particular commodity form, which has very little to do with the single text'. Ellis advanced a modified version of the argument which foregrounded 'segmentation' and 'repetition' as the main features of TV output. He suggested that the segment should be the basic unit of textual analysis, defining his concept with reference to selected examples – the thirty-second advertising spot, the isolated story in a news bulletin or the short scene from a television drama. In turn, the corresponding concept of repetition was used by Ellis to account for the recursive organisation of segments across space and time. He illustrated the widespread application of this principle in broadcasting by pointing to the most common of TV formats – series and serials. These are the industry's highly segmented, standardised products which return at the same place in the schedule day after day or week after week. In the case of a continuous serial – a soap opera – the fiction may be stretched over years and even decades, creating a strong sense of its own past and future (see Geraghty 1981).

Just as Williams's notion of flow was designed to account for the domestic experience of viewing as well as the aesthetics of television programming, so Ellis's arguments about the segmented and repetitive nature of TV output were tied to a series of reflections on the household context of reception. He described the television set itself as 'another domestic object, often the place where family photos are put – the direction of the glance towards the personalities on the TV screen being supplemented by the presence of "loved ones" immediately above' (Ellis 1982: 113). Broadcasting, unlike cinema, is 'intimate' and familiar – it is part of the furniture of ordinary daily life in private homes, rather than a site of spectacular public entertainment. For that reason, its symbolic products are tailored to meet the requirements of consumers who are routinely present yet typically 'distracted'. According to Ellis, this means TV tends to be a medium based much more on sound than the cinema is – constructing a 'regime of the glance' as opposed to the voyeuristic gaze of the film spectator at large-screen images in a darkened auditorium.

Of course, television makes available to its viewers a specific sort of 'look' at various happenings which take place in the world beyond the living room, but its modes of address and presentation are again shaped by the profoundly domestic character or feel of broadcasting:

> Broadcast TV creates a community of address in which viewer and TV institution ... look at the world that exists beyond them both. So TV is a relay, a kind of scanning apparatus that offers to present the world beyond the familiar and the familial, but to present it in a familiar and familial guise ... TV assumes that it has certain kinds of viewers ... that it speaks for them and looks for them. Interviewers base their questions on 'what the viewers at home want to know', drama bases itself on the notion of the family.
>
> (Ellis 1982: 163–5)

Perhaps the classic instance of that general process which Ellis described is TV news presentation. In this genre of broadcast output, viewers are invited to travel – imaginatively at least – to distant corners of the globe, witnessing what can often be quite disturbing events. However, the direct and seemingly personal address of the newsreader might best be seen as an attempt to reassure domestic consumers who are watching from their own local settings. The newsreader is a regular 'visitor' in the living room, 'bringing it all back home' to audiences.

First and foremost, the issues raised by my example are experiential ones. They have to do with the social role of television in mediating subjectivity – and in articulating private and public, or the local and the global, in particular ways. Any consideration of broadcasting as an institution in everyday life must take these experiential issues very seriously indeed. They are closely bound up with what Anthony Giddens (1990) has called a 'phenomenology of modernity', with the project of understanding how it feels to live day-to-day in late modern society. TV news is involved here in a dramatic reordering of traditional time-space relations, and has the potential to change previous patterns of familiarity and estrangement.

Secondly, though, Ellis's remarks concerning the look which television constructs for its viewers also lead us to ask crucial questions about the ideological power of broadcasting. He asserted that a complicity is continually being created between institution and audience. This bond, so the argument goes, is forged by addressing the viewer at home as 'you' – and by assuming a shared 'we position' from where several 'theys' may then be identified. A cultural distinction between insiders and outsiders is thereby produced – between social groups or constituencies which are placed either as the subjects or the objects of TV's look. The main difficulty with his otherwise sharp observations lies in the fact that not all audience members will necessarily take up their designated place within this ideological hailing and framing. As John Corner (1995: 19) put it in a recent commentary: 'Ellis's qualities as an alert critic of the medium ... fall victim to a familiar problem, that of extrapolating too freely from an analysis of a text's form to predictions about its social effects'.

Since the late 1970s, many researchers in the field of media and cultural studies have sought to avoid the problem which Corner identifies by investigating empirically the interpretative inter-actions between television and its audiences. The initial aim of this type of research was to plot the varied 'decodings' of audio-visual signs made by different audience groupings – to gauge the varying distances that their readings depart from those preferred meanings which get 'encoded' in texts at the point of production. Such distances are primarily social and semiotic but they rely upon spatio-temporal divisions too. For sociologist John Thompson (1988), a critical theory of ideology and mass communication has to try to incorporate each of these dimensions. So it is partly as a consequence of their extended availability in space and time that broadcasting's symbolic goods are open to 'differential interpretations' at the moment of reception and everyday use:

A distinctive characteristic of mass communication concerns ... the fact that the messages are potentially available to an extended audience which is altogether different from the interlocutors of a face-to-face interaction ... But the term 'mass' may be misleading ... For this term connotes not only a large quantity but also an indefinite shape, an inert, undifferentiated heap. However, the messages transmitted by the mass media are received by specific individuals in definite social-historical contexts. These individuals ... actively interpret and make sense of these messages and relate them to other aspects of their lives. This ongoing appropriation of media messages is an inherently critical and socially differentiated process ... there are systematic variations in their appropriation of media messages, variations which are linked to socially structured differences within the audience.

(Thompson 1988: 365–6)

For instance, when watching TV coverage of an industrial dispute, viewers might make sense of and respond to it in different ways – depending upon a combination of factors which are to do with their class position, social values and political allegiances. Similarly, soap operas may be enjoyed and appreciated by some yet despised and denigrated by others – chiefly because of variations in the age, gender or cultural competence of audience members. This is not to propose any crude 'sociological reductionism' where positions within the social structure are automatically assumed to determine patterns of meaning and taste. Nevertheless, the capacity actively to interpret and gain pleasure from broadcast output is inevitably constrained to some extent by our cultural backgrounds and belief systems. Knowledges and competences are unevenly distributed.

Thompson is rightly cautious about using the word 'mass' to describe communications between the producers and consumers of broadcast messages, but there could also be a question mark over our continued and taken-for-granted use of the term 'audience'. The plural, audiences, is preferable – denoting several groups divided either by their reception of various media and genres, or else by their social and cultural location – although a further conceptual difficulty still remains. Tracing the origins of this word, Janice Radway (1988) found that it once referred exclusively to an individual act of hearing in face-to-face verbal interaction. Only much later was it employed as a collective label for the absent receivers of electronically mediated communication. She points out how these two sets of circumstances are far from being equivalent. In the former, the producer and receiver of sound are co-present – they share a physical locale. If a valid comparison can be made with the theatre audience, where people are gathered together in a single place to give their attention to a stage performance, the parallel with watching television or listening to the radio is less clear. Here, as I stated at the outset, consumption practices are geographically dispersed across a multitude of settings and are frequently in competition with other domestic practices as a result of their embedding in day-to-day life. It therefore becomes harder to specify exactly where broadcasting's audiences begin and end. The boundaries of 'audiencehood' are inherently unstable. Radway's discussion certainly does invite us to be suspicious of any efforts to treat the audience unproblematically as a singular, stable entity. In the following section of this chapter, we shall see how similar doubts concerning the status of TV audiences as 'calculable objects' have led to a critique of the industry perspective on domestic consumption being launched by scholars in the field of media and cultural studies.

Before bringing this section to a close, though, I want to highlight an additional feature of the analytical model which Thompson has attempted to build. As well as advocating that we explore the significance of media messages as they are routinely appropriated and interpreted, he encourages us to consider 'the significance of the activity of reception' (Thompson 1988: 378) in its own right. His proposal owed much to the evolving research agenda of David Morley (1980; 1986), whose empirical work on television audiences had spanned both these areas of critical inquiry. So, after investigating the varied responses of viewing groups to selected segments from a popular current affairs programme, Morley proceeded to carry out further research on household contexts of consumption. 'My own interests are now focused on the "how" of television watching', he declared:

> This is to say that I ... prioritise the understanding of the process of television viewing ... the activity itself ... over the understanding of particular responses to particular types of programme material ... It is for this reason that ... the decision was taken to interview families ... in their homes − so as to get a better understanding of the ways in which television is watched in its 'natural' domestic context ... I would wish to argue that this is the necessary framework within which we must place our understanding of the particularity of individual responses to different types of programming.
>
> (Morley 1986: 41)

With this shift, Morley's previous concerns with the ideological power of the text and the meanings made by its readers were articulated to new interests in the interpersonal dynamics and 'cultural politics' of the viewing situation − a shift of focus which proved to be absolutely crucial for the study of broadcasting as an institution in everyday life.

## Ways of Addressing and Knowing Audiences

Ever since the early years of radio, broadcasters have faced the twin problems of how to address and gather knowledge about their dispersed and distant audiences. In the day-to-day production of programmes and the organisation of schedules, they were constantly having to ask themselves what was an appropriate way of speaking to their listeners at particular times and in particular domestic places. They were also in a position of knowing very little about the habits and size of their new listening public. In the intervening period, radio and later TV have gradually come to develop their own distinctive 'voices' or communicative styles for addressing the consumer in the private sphere, and have found specific ways of inquiring into audience behaviour – most notably through the manufacture of 'ratings' figures. In this part of the chapter, we look historically and critically at these key features of the industry's relationship to its audiences – its orientations towards viewers and listeners in the home environment. While most of the examples I draw on refer to British television and radio, there are references to literature on broadcast output and ratings research in the United States when it is deemed relevant to the issues being discussed.

## Intimacy at a Distance

We have already touched on Ellis's important assertions about the 'domesticity' of TV as a medium of communication – the familiar and intimate place of the technology and its symbolic forms in our daily lives – and in order to push those assertions further now, it is necessary for us to turn to some of the work done by historian and theorist of British public service broadcasting Paddy Scannell (1989; 1991a). Tracing the emergence of what he called the 'communicative ethos of broadcasting', Scannell (1989: 152) has remarked on the tendency of television and radio to employ increasingly 'relaxed ... and spontaneous modes of address and forms of talk'. Across a spread of programme types, from studio talk formats through to popular game shows, he detected the adoption of interactive styles which have traditionally been associated with more private interpersonal encounters – producing a universe of discourse that is designed to be experienced by audiences as ordinary, accessible and 'sociable'.

Of course, this feat was not accomplished overnight. Much of the talk to be heard on BBC radio until after the Second World War was marked by a certain degree of awkwardness or 'communicative unease'. An initially authoritarian mode of address, which was combined with a rather paternalist attitude towards the listener, gave way only later to 'a more populist and democratic manner and style' (Scannell 1991b: 10). The key to that change was a realisation that existing forms of public communication – such as the sermon, the lecture or the stage performance – were wholly inappropriate as models for the routine fare of broadcasting because of the space which separates producers from consumers in mediated interaction, and because of the private nature of reception contexts:

It was recognised that broadcast output, though articulated in the public domain as public discourse, was received within the sphere of privacy, as an optional leisure resource. Within this sphere ... people did not expect to be talked down to, lectured or 'got at'. They expected to be spoken to in a familiar, friendly and informal manner as if they were equals on the same footing as the speaker. The voices of radio and television ... are heard in the context of household activities and other household voices, as part of the general social arrangements of households and their members. It is this that powerfully drives the communicative style and manner of broadcasting to approximate to the norms not of public forms of talk, but to those of ordinary, informal conversation ... this is overwhelmingly the preferred communicative style of interaction between people in the routine contexts of day-to-day life and especially in the places where they live.

(Scannell 1991b: 3–4)

Although Scannell's chief concern as an analyst of public service broadcasting is with the gradual emergence of this communicative ethos in BBC output, it is no accident that the key moment of transformation which he points to here – from the late 1950s through into the 1960s – was also the period of ITV's arrival on the media landscape. The confident 'populist tone' of independent commercial TV was undoubtedly a significant factor in the shift towards a more sociable style of broadcasting in Britain (see Corner 1991).

Indeed, on the other side of the Atlantic, where television had established itself earlier, a number of the now common characteristics of broadcasting's address to audiences were already assuming a recognisable shape before the mid-1950s. Perhaps the most striking and distinctive of these was the direct address to camera in which TV show hosts and presenters spoke to consumers at home in an apparently personal way – what Donald Horton and Richard Wohl (1956) have termed 'para-social interaction'. This is the phrase they coined for that routine, taken-for-granted, yet quite remarkable encounter between small-screen personalities and domestic viewers – a serial interaction which takes place at a distance between public performers and their unknown audiences, but which 'simulates' many aspects of regular face-to-face conversation among friends or acquaintances. Despite the physical space that separates them, performers and viewers are brought together in live time, so that some of the immediacy of co-presence may be captured in circumstances of absence. As Horton and Wohl (1956: 215) observed, the television host often 'faces the spectator, uses the direct mode of address, talks as if ... conversing personally or privately'. Referring to popular American programmes of the day such as *The Steve Allen Show*, they believed an illusory yet deeply felt bond of intimacy was being formed in which loyal fans or devotees got to 'know' the personality. Not having monitored the actual responses of viewers to this direct mode of address, Horton and Wohl were in danger of assuming too much about audience identifications and pleasures. There are clearly questions concerning social patterns of identification that they failed to answer satisfactorily – questions to do with which viewing publics appreciate or dislike a particular 'persona' and screen performance. However, their analysis of para-social interaction contained extremely valuable insights into the developing presentational forms of TV.

John Langer (1981) picked up one of the main threads of their analysis in his article on television's 'personality system'. He examined the cultural roles played by 'those individuals constituted more or less exclusively for and by television, who make regular appearances as newsreaders, moderators, hosts, comperes or characters' (Langer 1981: 351). His writing revealed a sharp contrast between these figures and the representatives of the cinematic star system, providing further evidence of broadcasting's distinctive quotidian qualities:

> Whereas the star system operates from the realms of the spectacular, the inaccessible, the imaginary, presenting the cinematic universe as 'larger than life', the personality system is cultivated ... as 'part of life'; whereas the star system always has the ability to place distance between itself and its audiences through its insistence on 'the exceptional', the personality system works directly to construct and foreground intimacy and immediacy; whereas contact with stars is unrelentingly sporadic and uncertain, contact with television personalities has regularity and predictability; whereas stars are always playing 'parts' emphasising their identity as 'stars' as much – perhaps even more than – the characters they play, television personalities 'play' themselves ... personalities are distinguished ... for their typicality, their 'will to ordinariness'.
>
> (Langer 1981: 354–5)

Nowhere is this 'will to ordinariness' more evident than in the presentation of a 1990s daytime magazine such as *This Morning*. Transmitted on ITV between mid-morning and lunchtime each day during the week, the show has a highly segmented format with studio guests, phone-ins and various lifestyle features. Note that the programme title itself conveys a strong sense of immediacy – the 'here and now' of live TV – which is central to the communicative ethos of broadcasting. The husband-and-wife team who present the magazine are known and informally addressed by guests and phone-in callers as 'Richard and Judy'. Viewers are also expected to be on friendly, first-name terms with the personalities hosting the show.

*This Morning* actively constructs a simulation of domesticity by having the studio set furnished in the manner of a family living room. The two presenters and their guests sit in armchairs beside a coffee table. To reinforce this relaxed household atmosphere, their celebrity guests are thanked for 'dropping in' or invited to 'visit again'. At certain pivotal moments in the magazine show, the personalities' para-social relationship with audiences has to be established and regularly re-established. The initial encounters at the start of each broadcast, the points at which viewers are returned to the studio after some kind of break or video insert, along with closing farewells at the finish – all offer an opportunity for the hosts to talk directly to camera in a casual fashion. The typical greetings and partings uttered by Richard and Judy – 'morning to you', 'hiya', 'bye' and 'see you tomorrow' – reflect a far wider process of change in late modern society that Norman Fairclough (1994) has named a 'conversationalisation of public discourse'. A key characteristic of this cultural trend is what he referred to as 'synthetic personalisation', the simulation of a personal relation between a text and an audience.

Other instances of synthetic personalisation and performed 'sincerity' in broadcasting can be found in a long tradition of programmes which could best be described as 'people shows'. This is because they involve different sorts of face-to-face interaction between a television or radio personality and ordinary members of the general public – who also appear momentarily as personalities in front of the camera or microphone – as well as para-social interaction with dispersed domestic audiences. I have in mind Wilfred Pickles presenting *Have a Go!* on BBC radio in the 1950s, and contemporary figures such as Cilla Black on *Blind Date* and Michael Barrymore in *My Kind of People* on ITV in the 1990s. Each of these personalities has made their name in broadcasting not through being extraordinary, but precisely by seeming to viewers to be familiar, homely and down-to-earth. In chat shows and studio discussions, too, there have been similar TV performers whose own names often provided the programme's title – *Wogan, Kilroy!, Esther, Vanessa* and so on. All have presented themselves to viewers as being 'of the people', asking common-sense questions 'on our behalf'. From the United States, meanwhile, come programmes which have helped to shape and define those popular genres of studio talk – *Donahue*, *The Oprah Winfrey Show* and *Ricki Lake*.

## Behind the Ratings

This long search to find suitable modes of address and forms of talk was accompanied by a parallel quest on the part of broadcasting organisations to devise particular ways of researching and 'knowing' their audiences. By the mid-1930s, the BBC had set up a Listener Research Department to help improve the quality of its service to the public – although its precise aims and methods of inquiry were, according to David Chaney (1987: 272), rather poorly defined at the outset: 'Not only was the relevance of research accepted only cautiously ... but those concerned were not consistent about what they hoped to do or what ... could be accomplished'. No such doubts were in evidence when listener research took off in the United States. From the end of the 1920s onwards, ratings figures compiled by market research agencies became the industry's primary measure of performance in the context of a commercial broadcasting system where it was necessary to demonstrate the existence of an audience to potential advertisers or sponsors. As Dallas Smythe (1981) once put it in a provocative and memorable phrase, broadcasting which operates under market conditions is in the business of 'delivering audiences to advertisers'. To ensure its economic survival and prosperity, the industry must fill the spots within and between radio and television programmes. Following that logic, programmes themselves are merely the bait to attract consumers to the advertisements. While symbolic goods manufactured by commercial broadcasters are commodities of a sort, it is ultimately the sale of the 'audience commodity' which is crucial in financial terms.

On both sides of the Atlantic now, principles of audience measurement are central to the kind of research conducted and commissioned on behalf of the industry – either by agencies such as Nielsen in America or by the Broadcasters' Audience Research Board in Britain, a body jointly funded by the BBC and various commercial TV companies. Despite the continued use of qualitative scales such as viewer 'appreciation indices', it is quantitative data on audience size that currently dominates industry thinking. However, this specific way of thinking and constructing knowledge about television viewing has recently been subjected to a radical critique which comes from outside the institutional framework of broadcasting – notably in the writings of media and cultural studies academic Ien Ang (1991; 1992). She recognised that the ratings are institutionally enabling, a necessary 'fiction' for the broadcasters, but also believed them to be epistemologically limited. In other words, they can serve a useful economic function for the industry and yet offer only a partial representation of everyday TV consumption. The story which Ang tells in her work on institutional audience research is of an industry's ongoing desire to convert the elusive occurrence of real people watching television into a known, objectified category. This narrative features an increasingly desperate quest to come up with the perfect technical fix, a 'panoptic' measurement technology that might be able to monitor the movement of viewers in front of the screen at every moment of the day and night – thereby revealing the exact size and demographic shape of a TV audience to broadcasters and advertisers.

Initially, the technique of audience measurement was quite simple – a questionnaire survey carried out by brief telephone or street interviews. Later, ratings figures were calculated on the basis of data gathered from electronic 'set meters' and diary entries in a chosen 'panel' of households. These panels were samples which had been designed to stand for the viewing population as a whole. Their programme choices were supposedly generalisable – resulting in the claim that a given number of people, counted in their millions, watched a particular television broadcast. The set meter gave an accurate statement to researchers of when the TV was switched on and off, and when channels were changed in the panel homes. A diary served as a supplementary source of data, with household members being asked to keep a written record of their personal viewing habits.

More recently, though, ratings researchers have acknowledged some of the problems associated with these established methods and procedures. Diaries depended upon viewers in the panel homes filling them in conscientiously, and knowing whether a set is switched on is not the same thing as knowing whether anyone is actually looking at the screen. As we know from our own experiences of daily domestic life, 'watching television' is not always a clear-cut activity. Instead, it is frequently done in combination with a range of other tasks – such as reading the newspaper, holding a conversation or eating a meal – so that TV has to compete for space and time in the household context. The response of those whose job it is to measure audiences has not been to register the full complexity of situated viewing practices by turning to more qualitative methods of investigation. Rather they continue undaunted in their efforts to transform the complex into the concrete and the calculable, producing a plausible fiction for sale to advertisers.

Faced with the vagaries of domestic consumption, and with viewers who are regularly 'zapping' around multi-channel broadcasting systems or else 'zipping' through video-recorded material, industry and market researchers in both Britain and the United States have now developed an audience measurement technology called the 'people meter'. Designed to monitor individual viewing habits within the panel home, it combines the previous functions of set meter and diary in an integrated electronic gadget:

> When a viewer begins to watch a programme, (s)he must press a numbered button on a portable keypad, which looks like the well known remote control device. When a viewer stops watching, the button must be pressed again. A monitor attached to the television set lights up regularly to remind the viewer of the button-pushing task. Every member of a sample family has her or his own individual button, while there are also some extra buttons for guests.
>
> (Ang 1992: 137)

Doubts about the co-operation of consumers in using the gadget remain, however, and this has led to the piloting of a further innovation – known as a 'passive people meter'. Here, the necessity for a human hand to intervene is apparently eliminated altogether. The passive people meter is an image-recognition device fitted to the television set. It is capable of recording precisely which faces in the living room are directed towards the screen. Of course, it cannot tell us what sense viewers might be making of what they see and do, but it does promise finally to realise the dreams of ratings agencies for a panoptic system of audience surveillance.

'Surveillance' may seem far too strong a term in this particular context, with all the connotations of discipline and control that it carries (see Foucault 1977) – yet Ang uses it with exactly those connotations in mind. She comprehends this sort of quantitative research on TV viewing as an attempt by the industry to impose a degree of order on what is an increasingly undisciplined and elusive set of cultural practices. The audience for broadcasting is understood as an object which is constituted by the ratings rather than as a pre-given entity. Within the terms of her critique, there is no such thing as the television audience – at least not in any coherent, homogeneous form – although she stops short of arguing that there is nothing outside of institutional categories, retaining a crucial place in her analysis for the 'social world of actual audiences'.

That world is the realm of day-to-day life and household cultures of consumption. It does not lend itself to being measured because it exists as a dispersed domain of lived experiences and cultural meanings – not as a calculable object. For this reason, in order for us to get 'behind the ratings' (Morley 1990) to explore these experiences and meanings, we have to adopt methods with very different purposes:

> The kind of research that needs doing would involve identifying and investigating ... the differences behind the catch all category of 'watching television'. We all watch television ... but with how much attention and with what degree of commitment, in relation to which types of programmes and occasions? ... Research needs to investigate the complex ways in which television is embedded in a ... range of everyday practices.
>
> (Morley 1990: 8)

In the next section of the chapter, I consider several examples of work in media and cultural studies which has attempted to answer the sorts of question posed in the passage above. Researchers working in this field have adopted what can be described as an ethnographic approach to the social world of actual audiences – usually involving conversational interviews with consumers and observations of their routine reception contexts. So whereas ratings agencies construct a profitable audience commodity through techniques of measurement, reception ethnographers are trying instead to produce rich and detailed accounts of media consumption which are sensitive to the dynamics of interpretation, taste and power – sensitive, in other words, to the qualitative aspects of reception or the 'politics' of the living room. Like the ratings figures, the words that they write will be 'partial truths' (Clifford 1986) – but ones which seek to represent the point of view of audiences.

## The Social Relations of Viewing and Listening

As we turn our critical attention now to the social relations of viewing and listening in broadcast communication, let us start by recalling a couple of interrelated points that were made earlier when I was commenting on Thompson's social theory of the media (Thompson 1988; 1994). First, media messages have an extended availability in space and time – this is one of the reasons why they are open to being differentially received and appropriated – and, for Thompson (1994: 44), the process of appropriation is structured yet selective and creative: 'individuals draw on the resources available to them in order to ... make sense of the symbolic material transmitted by the media'. Secondly, he noted that there are two dimensions to an act of cultural consumption – the meanings and pleasures which are generated in semiotic encounters between a text and a reader, and the significance that reception practices themselves have in everyday locations. Each of those important points is taken up and developed further here, with reference to selected examples from the literature.

## Interpretation and Taste

An initial attempt in media and cultural studies to conceptualise the interpretation of broadcast messages by distant audiences was Stuart Hall's model of encoding and decoding in the TV discourse (Hall 1973). His model was designed to deal principally with the ideological dimensions of broadcasting. It drew partly on existing theories of meaning production in semiotics, but also on accounts of social structure and cultural reproduction from the sociological tradition. He sought to explain, on the one hand, how television texts are constructed so as to 'prefer' a particular dominant reading of social events. This is not the result of a conscious bias of the broadcasters, more a taken-for-granted set of assumptions about how the world is to be represented. On the other hand, Hall wanted to account for the engagement of actual readers with the encoded representations which are offered to them by TV. His contention was that the varied class positions and cultural knowledges of viewers and listeners are likely to generate differential responses to and interpretations of broadcast texts. Depending on what it is they bring with them to the message, their readings will vary. Hall tentatively identified three hypothetical positions from which decodings of a television text might be made – 'dominant', 'negotiated' and 'oppositional'. In short, the first involves an acceptance of the preferred reading, the second allows a limited challenge to it on matters of local detail, while the third entails a wholesale rejection of the dominant definitions on offer, often accompanied by an effort to provide alternative ones.

Morley (1980) was later to adopt and adapt this conceptual framework in an empirical research project that set out to analyse the decodings of a TV news magazine which were made by groups consisting of managers, students, apprentices or trade unionists. In all, Morley conducted interviews with twenty-nine such groups in educational institutions, before using Hall's categories as a way of classifying their differential interpretations of recorded extracts from the programme. For instance, he found that management groups, schoolboys and apprentices inhabited the dominant decoding position and accepted the meaning preferred by the text. Negotiated readings were made by teacher training and university arts students. Trade union groups, depending on their members' roles as either full-time officials or shop stewards, produced versions of a negotiated or oppositional decoding. Meanwhile, the black further education college students interviewed in his study were constructing oppositional readings of another kind altogether – not so much contesting the preferred view of the world offered by the programme as 'refusing' to engage with current affairs coverage that had little relevance to them.

Ultimately, though, Morley felt constrained by the categories he had inherited from Hall. They lacked the subtlety required to cope with certain contradictions which arose in an analysis of the group responses. So, for example, bank managers who occupied a dominant decoding position were nevertheless dismissive of the populist style in which events and issues were presented. The reverse was also the case for groups of trade unionists – while some respondents were willing to endorse the presentational style of the programme, the shop stewards forcefully rejected what they perceived to be its right-wing political sympathies and its failure to tackle fundamental questions about class and economics. There are evident difficulties in trying to hold on to both of those dimensions of decoding at once. What the interviewees said, or did not say, to the researcher was only partly concerned with distances taken from a preferred reading – the stances they adopted in relation to specific ideological propositions or framings. The responses of the bank managers and trade unionists clearly had just as much to do with patterns of taste and preference. Indeed, it may have been a little premature to ask how the text was interpreted when several of Morley's research subjects did not routinely watch the early evening programme that he was inviting them to discuss.

This led him to propose, in his critical postscript to the project (Morley 1981), a more 'genre-based' model of media consumption which could focus its attention on the 'salience' of particular types of text for particular sorts of reader – and on the cultural competences necessary for viewers and listeners to be able to understand and enjoy various genres of broadcast output. It would, he stated, 'involve us in dealing more with the relevance/irrelevance and comprehension/incomprehension dimensions of decoding rather than being directly concerned with the acceptance or rejection of substantive ideological themes' (Morley 1981: 10). A consequence of his modified approach was that pleasure and displeasure were to be investigated as complex social accomplishments. In other words, our likes and dislikes are not just to be approached as a matter of personal taste – rather, they are related to our position in the social structure. It was recognised that enjoyment of a given television or radio programme requires an articulation of certain generic forms and preoccupations with those unevenly distributed stocks of 'cultural capital' (Bourdieu 1984) which different audiences and taste publics possess.

Much of the subsequent research on decoding went on to examine issues of gender and genre – choosing to look, for instance, at women's engagements with soap opera. Carried out in the main by feminist researchers in media and cultural studies, this work was often motivated by a political desire to 'rescue' previously denigrated feminine pleasures, and to demonstrate the highly skilled and discriminating nature of fans' preferences. Writing in a journal known then for its championing of avant-garde 'art house' cinema, Charlotte Brunsdon (1981: 36) suggested somewhat controversially that the competent soap opera viewer deserves to be treated as seriously as the film buff:

> Just as a Godard film requires the possession of certain forms of cultural capital on the part of its audience ... an extra-textual familiarity with ... artistic, linguistic, political and cinematic discourses – so too does soap opera ... It is the culturally constructed skills of femininity – sensitivity, perception, intuition and the necessary privileging of the concerns of personal life – which are both called on and practised in the genre.

Ethnographies which try to re-evaluate positively the pleasures of popular TV – producing what Brunsdon (1989) was later to call a 'redemptive reading' – can run the risk of celebrating subordinated experiences uncritically. The dangers of 'going native' are great. Equally great, though, is the importance of mapping gendered distinctions in media consumption. It enabled feminist critics to open up a politics of cultural taste and value, shaking the foundations of established aesthetic judgement and giving an authentic voice to viewing communities that had been mocked or silenced in the past.

The work of Dorothy Hobson (1982) on the now defunct serial *Crossroads* is a good case in point. She visited the homes of female fans, watching an episode of the programme and getting into discussion with them about the characters and storylines. Her research revealed an intriguing mix of feelings among these women about their favourite programme. They were able to talk at considerable length about what it was they enjoyed, but they were also deeply conscious of the low status which their pleasures had in the wider cultural economy – leading many to be either apologetic or defensive. So some seemed to accept, with reluctance, the dismissive judgements of *Crossroads* being made by husbands and by television critics – yet others were well aware that they had a rich stock of feminine skills at their disposal. This awareness is neatly expressed in the following extract from the interview transcripts: 'Men ... think it's just stupid and unrealistic because they are not brought up to accept emotional situations ... They don't like it 'cos it's sometimes sentimental ... I don't know any men who watch it' (Hobson 1982: 109).

Of course, we must be careful not to reduce cultural distinctions of this kind to an essential biological difference between the sexes. Feminist theorists in media and cultural studies have been keen to stress that gendered identifications with different genres of broadcast output are always socially constructed and historically contingent. The list of skills which Brunsdon presents us with above – sensitivity, perception, intuition and a privileging of 'the personal' – is not a catalogue of 'natural' female attributes but a recognition that, under present cultural circumstances, many women have made a heavy investment in the sphere of 'emotionally significant interaction' (Brunsdon 1981). It would be possible for a biological male to occupy the same imaginative realm. In practice, given current masculine discourses and subjectivities, men rarely do. Instead, the masculine domain of TV is more typically populated by news and current affairs, or by sport and 'realist' fiction (Morley 1986).

It is interesting that men should dismiss classic soap opera on occasion as 'unrealistic', because women who enjoy the genre will frequently say they like it precisely for its 'true to life' qualities. This was what Ang (1985) found when she analysed letters which were sent to her by Dutch followers of the globally distributed American serial *Dallas*. Many of the correspondents indicated that their enjoyment of the programme was derived from its relevance to everyday experience. For example, 'I like watching it ... because ... it's really ordinary daily problems more than anything that occur in it and that you recognise ... the characters reflect the daily life of a family' (Ang 1985: 43).

Bearing in mind the obvious imbalance between the Ewings' extravagant lifestyle at Southfork and the day-to-day domestic conditions of television viewers in Holland, we might be surprised initially – as Ang was – to find *Dallas* being understood in quite this way. She faced the predicament of how to account for the puzzling claims of her letter writers, who were responding to fictional representations produced on the other side of the Atlantic. Her solution was to introduce the concept of 'emotional realism'. She saw that the correspondents were empathising with the characters and situations in what is basically a family tragedy. A powerful emotional resonance rendered the fiction real and pleasurable for them.

As melodrama, *Dallas* embodies what Ang named the 'tragic structure of feeling'. Whereas British and Australian soap operas are sometimes ridiculed for their lack of dramatic action, critics of American serials like this one usually accuse them of the exact opposite – of overplaying sensational incident. In the life of the Ewing family, then, there is a literally unbelievable procession of major events and crises – but the deliberate purpose of these exaggerated plot lines is to heighten emotional tension. Dismissing the programme as 'overdone' is to miss the point completely. *Dallas* strives to stir the passions with its continual round of remarkable happenings. Whether or not audiences are duly stirred depends on the dispositions which are brought to the text by its readers:

> The tragic structure of feeling, which is inscribed in the meaning structure of *Dallas*, will not automatically and obviously agree with the meanings viewers apply ... That will only happen if they are sensitive to it. In other words, the tragic structure of feeling ... will only make sense if one can ... project oneself onto, i.e. recognise, a 'melodramatic imagination'. Viewers must therefore have a certain ... orientation to understand and evaluate *Dallas* in a melodramatic way.
>
> (Ang 1985: 79)

Ang suggests that this melodramatic imagination is a predominantly feminine recognition. She notes that it emerges out of a willingness to face 'life's torments' from a particular emotional standpoint. It results in a vicarious identification with characters such as Sue Ellen and Miss Ellie – a wife driven to drink by a scheming husband and a mother who carries the worries of the whole family on her shoulders. Both are seen as 'really human' by several of the women who wrote letters to the researcher.

However, popular programmes like *Dallas* have obviously not gone out to a wholly female audience. Ang acknowledged that there must be pleasures in the text which are on offer to men as well. Speculating about possible masculine readings, she wondered whether their enjoyment might have come more from a recognition of 'the business relations and problems, the cowboy elements, and the power and wealth represented' (Ang 1985: 118). Her suspicion was that male viewers are unlikely to have the same orientation towards the tragic structure of feeling. In a survey of prime-time soaps, Christine Geraghty (1991) traces the growing trend of introducing narrative features into the continuous serial which are familiar from other genres. To widen the appeal of their programmes, producers are bringing in a broader range of male characters – developing plot lines reminiscent of crime series or else working with sports themes. *Brookside* and *EastEnders* may be read as examples of this 'defeminisation' process.

## Power in Domestic Cultures

While the literature on interpretation and taste which I discuss above encourages us to examine social constructions of meaning and pleasure in media consumption, we need to consider further the significance that reception practices themselves have in our everyday lives, or the 'how' of viewing and listening in domestic cultures. This means reflecting on the household uses of TV and radio as technologies, asking about their status as objects in the home alongside their role as providers of broadcast output. It is also necessary for us to think about how communication technologies are embedded in the interpersonal dynamics and power relations of life in the private sphere. One of the difficulties which we face in doing this is that broadcasting is so much a taken-for-granted part of modern domestic experience – an institution in everyday life – and it is therefore not easy to distance ourselves enough to explore its significance in routine situations. A way around the problem is to chart the historical formation of broadcasting's relationship with the home, and my own oral history research on the entry and incorporation of early radio into household settings in the 1920s and 1930s was an attempt to begin that mapping (see Chapter 3). For now, though, I review the work of some other researchers who have employed qualitative research methods in an attempt to remark on the seemingly unremarkable practices of daily viewing and listening.

For instance, Hermann Bausinger (1984) in Germany has observed how turning on the television can signify very different things depending upon the context of the act and the intentions of the person who is switching it on. In certain circumstances, it might mean 'I want to watch this', but at other times it could equally be signalling 'I would like to hear and see nothing'. James Lull (1990) has referred to similar sorts of mundane activity as tactics of affiliation and avoidance. His typology of the social uses of TV in the home is extremely valuable in highlighting numerous 'relational uses' to which the technology is put by its consumers, and here he was arguing that television may serve either as a basis for a shared occasion or as an excuse for not communicating with fellow family members at all.

Lull was interested, too, in how families select TV programmes to watch. This is potentially an indicator of power relations within a household, especially if there are clashes of taste and preference. Reporting on research carried out during the 1980s in the United States, he concluded:

> The locus of control in the programme selection process can be explained primarily by family position ... In this study ... data converged to demonstrate convincingly that fathers had more perceived and actual control of the selection of television programmes than any other individual in the family. Mothers were the least influential family members in this regard.
>
> (Lull 1990: 93)

The same conclusions were reached independently by Morley (1986; 1988) in Britain following conversational interviews which he taped at the homes of eighteen families from a district of south London. A limitation of his previous decoding study had been its failure to situate viewers' interpretations of television in the settings of domestic life, and this follow-up research was designed to explore precisely that – to track down the meanings of the medium at the usual site of reception. So the purpose of Morley's conversations with consumers was to supply data for an analysis of TV reception as a routine 'social event'. Looking at the interview transcripts, he saw a consistency of response around gender differences – dealing with the question of power and control over programme choice beside other issues which were to do with divisions of labour and leisure in households, or with varied styles of television viewing.

At the heart of Morley's analysis was an observation that the men and women he talked with actually had quite different feelings about the homes they lived in. For husbands, the private sphere was primarily a site of leisure – defined in opposition to a public workplace – but for the wives, even those with paid employment elsewhere, it was a space in which they were rarely if ever 'off duty' (see Deem 1986). This disparity in their 'relative freedoms' to partake in domestic entertainment led to a gap between masculine and feminine viewing styles. So whereas the men expressed a desire to watch quietly and attentively, women were typically obliged to participate in a more distracted form of TV consumption. Their reported viewing habits usually involved the performance of other domestic activities, such as ironing or sewing, at the same time as keeping half an eye on the screen. The researcher found that the television remote control device used to switch channels was a potent symbol of patriarchal power in these families. In discussing his data, Morley (1986: 148) referred to this object as 'the symbolic possession of the father ... used almost exclusively by him'. It was located on the arm of 'dad's chair'.

Morley admitted that there were also some limitations to this follow-up study. It focused exclusively on traditional 'nuclear' family units in which both parents lived together with their dependent children. In addition, all were white, lower middle-class or working-class homes in a specific urban area. This led the researcher to be cautious about the generalisability of his findings, claiming them 'to be representative, at most, of viewing patterns within one type of household, drawn from one particular ethnic and geographic context and from a relatively narrow range of class positions' (Morley 1986: 11). Having said that, gender is a significant variable in the vast majority of domestic cultures – even if the gendered practices and dynamics of other household types may differ.

With the benefit of hindsight, we can now add a further qualification to those listed by Morley – the historical specificity of his findings. Back in the mid-1980s when he carried out that research, it was far more common for a household to have a single TV set around which struggles for control of family viewing would take place. Today, though, many of us live in homes where there is multiple set ownership and where other screens – personal computers and video games – compete with television for our attention. The home is becoming a 'cellular' media environment, with the consumption and use of communication technologies taking increasingly fragmented and individualised forms. Even so, power relations in domestic settings remain a pressing issue. There are questions about who gets to watch the main set in the living room and who makes do with a smaller screen in the bedroom or kitchen.

On a final note in this section, I want to consider whether Morley's investigation is centrally concerned with broadcasting after all, or whether his work here takes us in the direction of a broader sociology of the family. TV viewing certainly gives him a good 'way in' to the private domain, a convenient point of departure – but maybe we could conclude that the emphasis he puts on processes of domestic interaction and on divisions of labour and leisure transcends any narrow interest in media audiences. If our objective is to comprehend television's 'embedding' in everyday household life (Silverstone 1990), then the boundaries of reception studies – like the boundaries of audiencehood itself – become increasingly unstable. In fact, there are striking parallels between the stories told by Morley's interviewees and remarks made by women in an ethnography of family food consumption carried out by Nickie Charles and Marion Kerr (1988).

Just as in Morley's sample, which contained homes where men had the symbolic power to control programme choice, so Charles and Kerr found that the content of meals in households they visited was often determined by masculine tastes. Feminine culinary preferences were less conservative – wives were willing to try out new flavours and 'foreign' dishes – but the husbands' demands for so-called 'proper meals' limited what was served up at the dining table. The voices of the women quoted below clearly echo those recorded by Morley:

> My husband is very traditional-minded about food ... so I tend to stick to the same thing most weeks – I rarely buy anything just for myself ... I'd like to eat all sorts of foods, foreign foods, but I don't bother ... I forgo it ... If I cook something that's got a whiff of herbs in it he'll put his knife and fork down and say, 'I'm sorry but I'm not eating it' ... He usually waits until ... I've prepared something a bit out of the ordinary, and he'll leave it. I'm not happy but there again I'll not make a scene. I'm not one for rowing ... I cook what I know he will like ... I mean I won't try things knowing he won't like them. Things like pasta, I know he won't eat that, so I don't cook it.
>
> (Charles and Kerr 1988: 70–2)

Gendered relationships to the two domestic technologies involved – a TV remote control device and a kitchen cooker – are obviously different. Men dominate use of the former and delegate responsibility for operating the latter to women, yet the same basic dynamic is revealed in each of these separate research projects. Where there is a clash of tastes it is masculine preferences which tend to prevail, while women feel that their social position as wife and mother requires them to exercise a degree of 'self-denial'.

Exceptions to this general rule in Morley's study were specific instances where women took the opportunity to indulge in the 'guilty pleasures' of a solo viewing, managing to escape temporarily from their ongoing duties as wives and mothers by watching a film on video or a favourite television serial when the rest of the family were out of the way: 'If I'm here alone, I try to get something a bit mushy and then I sit ... and have a cry ... I enjoy that ... I get one of those love stories if he's not in ... Yes, it's on his nights out. It doesn't happen very often' (Morley 1986: 160). In direct parallel, Charles and Kerr (1988: 71) discovered an example of what we might call the guilty pleasures of a 'solo serving': 'I have a passion for spaghetti and butter, that kind of thing, which nobody else in the family likes, so occasionally I do that ... when I'm on my own'.

## Senses of Identity and Formations of Community

If my comparison between TV viewing and food consumption helps us to see how broadcasting's audiences are caught up in a con-textual web of domestic relations, we must remember what it is that distinguishes media technologies from other objects in the house-hold setting. Through sound and image, broadcasting serves to connect the private sphere of the home with various public worlds beyond the front door, mediating our senses of personal and collec-tive identity. Television and radio provide us with routine access to flows of communication and information which can be appropriated in what Giddens (1991) has named the 'reflexive project of the self'. Broadcasting also brings us into intimate contact with events in far-away locations and makes available different identifications with its 'territories of transmission' at a regional, national or transnational level. In this last section of the chapter, I search for ways of explain-ing those changing connections between the local and the global, exploring the consequences for formations of self and community.

### The Mediation of Experience

Giddens (1990; 1991) offered an account of modern institutions and ways of living which deals precisely with the shifting relations between local cultures and globalising processes. His social theory of modernity explains how the small details of personal experience and self-identity are now inextricably bound up with large-scale institutional and technological transformations, so that one of the main aims of his work was to try to understand how it feels to live in the modern age – to comprehend what has been described, in media and cultural studies, as the 'subjective side' of social change (see Johnson 1986). Giddens demonstrated a deep concern, then, with experiential or phenomenological issues – yet he insisted on approaching them with reference to broader historical questions about the distinctive character of contemporary society.

As I discussed briefly in Chapter 1, the starting point for Giddens's notes on experience and self-identity in conditions of late modernity was an argument which had to do with the extension of space and time beyond the confines of place. He asserted that, in the transition to and the growth of a modern society, social relationships have increasingly been 'lifted out' of situated locales and stretched across often vast geographical distances – resulting in a disembedding of social systems. In addition, not only are relations with others no longer contained within a bounded locale, but daily life is now touched and 'penetrated' to a much greater extent by distant forces. The various disembedding mechanisms of modernity – what Giddens (1990) called its 'symbolic tokens' and 'expert systems' – along with the emergence of modern media technologies, have served to alter significantly our experiences of being in the world:

> The influence of distant happenings on ... intimacies of the self ... becomes more and more commonplace. The media, printed and electronic, obviously play a central role in this respect ... With the development of mass communication, particularly electronic communication, the interpenetration of self-development and social systems, up to and including global systems, becomes ever more pronounced. The 'world' in which we now live is in some profound respects thus quite distinct from that inhabited by human beings in previous periods of history.
>
> (Giddens 1991: 4–5)

Our experiences are no longer place-bound in quite the same way as they once were prior to the arrival of electronic media in the twentieth century. Many of the materials which we draw upon in order to construct senses of personal identity are mediated.

This is certainly not to suggest that local experience and face-to-face interaction have ceased to be important in the formation of the modern self. Despite the potential for access to global networks of communication and information, there is still a powerful 'compulsion of proximity' (Boden and Molotch 1994) in contemporary culture. It is also the case that those immediate contacts which we develop with family, friends and colleagues continue to shape our senses of who we are and our subjective outlooks on the world. Rather, the task here for social and cultural theory is to think through the nature of the articulation between local and mediated experience in the day-to-day routines and biographies of social subjects.

John Thompson (1995: 233) expressed exactly what is at stake when he wrote about the changing 'interaction mix' of modern life, and the fashioning of self and experience in technologically mediated cultural environments:

> Living in a mediated world involves a constant interweaving of different forms of experience ... we think of ourselves and our life trajectories primarily in relation to the others whom, and the events which, we encounter ... in the practical contexts of our daily lives. However ... mediated experience ... assumes a greater and greater role in the process of self-formation. Individuals increasingly draw on mediated experience to inform and refashion the project of the self.

His notion of the self as a symbolic project was borrowed from Giddens's social theory – and, for Giddens, self-identity had to do with the capacity to keep a particular narrative going. Individuals make use of the symbolic resources which are available as they struggle to maintain an ongoing 'story' about the self. For example, he contended that the serial form in broadcasting can provide its viewers with 'a feeling of coherent narrative which is a reassuring balance to difficulties in sustaining the narrative of the self in actual social situations' (Giddens 1991: 199). More generally, though, the argument is that we each act as our own 'unofficial biographer' – trying to produce a meaningful story with a past, present and future. The kinds of story being told will inevitably differ, as there is only a limited range of 'scripts' accessible to us in our specific cultural circumstances, but the wider principles of autobiographical narration are common in the late modern era.

A further significant feature of self-formation, according to Giddens and Thompson, is the highly reflexive nature of this project. Narrating personal identity requires us constantly to monitor our routine activities and to reflect on various lifestyle options. Indeed, modernity is characterised by a distinctive type of institutional reflexivity, where the knowledge produced about social life becomes a constitutive element in its organisation and transformation. For instance, we might consider how information circulated in the public domain concerning global ecological issues can impact on the local purchasing decisions of private individuals who revise their day-to-day practices in the light of this flow of communication. The same goes for knowledge and advice – distributed via TV and radio – about health matters, or else how to cope with emotional problems. These broadcast discourses are selectively and reflexively appropriated by viewers and listeners as they monitor their lifestyles and interpersonal relationships.

## Electronic Landscapes

So far in this final section, I have concentrated on the making of personal rather than collective identities, although the theorists whose work we have looked at clearly see the self as a social product which is fashioned at the interface between private lives and public cultures. I now want us to focus on formations of modern community in greater detail. Many aspects of the analysis presented above are still relevant here, especially those insights offered by Giddens into the ordering of space and time, and the disembedding of social systems. Whereas pre-modern communities were chiefly organised around a fixed place or location, mediated experience has meant that contemporary community is increasingly stretched across spatial distances, yet held together in conditions of temporal simultaneity. The institution and technologies of broadcasting are therefore central to our changing senses of collective identity.

Communities might best be understood as 'fictional realities'. They appear to have an objective existence, but are actually products of the imagination. In his book on the origin and spread of nationalism, historian Benedict Anderson (1983) has adopted this line of argument, referring to nations themselves as imagined communities. A short passage in Anderson's book which is of particular interest to us concerns the symbolic function of media consumption in the 'fictioning' of nationhood. He commented there on the ritual act of reading the newspaper, taking it to be a sign of the individual consumer's participation in an 'extraordinary mass ceremony':

> The significance of this mass ceremony ... is paradoxical. It is performed in silent privacy, in the lair of the skull. Yet each communicant is well aware that the ceremony he performs is being replicated simultaneously by thousands or millions of others of whose existence he is confident ... Furthermore, this ceremony is incessantly repeated at daily or half-daily intervals throughout the calendar. What more vivid figure for the ... historically clocked, imagined community can be envisioned? At the same time, the newspaper reader, observing exact replicas of his own paper being consumed ... is continually reassured that the imagined world is rooted in everyday life ... creating that remarkable confidence of

> community in anonymity which is the hallmark of modern
> nations.
>
> (Anderson 1983: 35)

The same sort of confidence of community in anonymity was
available to audiences for public service broadcasting in Britain
with the arrival of radio and, later, television (Cardiff and Scannell
1987). In fact, that experience of simultaneous reception described
by Anderson was probably heightened with the coming of broadcasting. Programmes were heard or seen live by absent millions
who were dispersed in their domestic settings. They were thereby
invited to identify with a wider 'general public' – to imagine
themselves as members of a national community which was then
reproduced by TV and radio day in day out, week in week out, and
year in year out.

Today, however, this traditional feeling of confidence in the
existence of the nation as a shared community is not so readily
available from broadcasting. Of course, the BBC continues to
provide its viewers and listeners with common access to a
schedule of national programming – but by the 1990s, several
factors have contributed to a shift in the imaginative geography of
community and in broadcasting's electronic landscapes (Morley
and Robins 1995). Alongside general changes in the spatio-
temporal organisation of modern institutions – like the international scale of commerce and politics, and the expanding reach
of telecommunication and transportation networks – we are witnessing a trend towards the 'transnationalisation' or globalisation
of audio-visual industries and their audiences. The deregulation
of broadcasting, more accurately its 're-regulation' (Corner et al.
1994), and the introduction of new technologies for cable and
satellite transmission have led to a greater level of competition
between television companies. Indeed, media policy decisions
have helped to bring about a marked decline in the influence of
national public service broadcasting in Western European
countries:

> The political and social concerns of the public service era ...
> with national culture and identity ... have come to be
> regarded as factors inhibiting the development of new media
> markets ... Driven now by the logic of profit and competition,
> the overriding objective of the new media corporations is to
> get their product to the largest number of consumers. There is
> ... an expansionist tendency at work, pushing ceaselessly
> towards the construction of enlarged audio-visual spaces and

markets. The imperative is to break down the old frontiers of national communities ... Audio-visual geographies are thus becoming detached from the symbolic spaces of national culture ... The new media order is set to become a global order.

(Morley and Robins 1995: 11)

In these changed economic circumstances, a crucial question is how viewers in local situations are responding to global shifts. Any discussion of the impact of new TV technologies and territories of transmission must be set in the context of everyday domestic practices. It is necessary for us to enter the private sphere of the home, in order to ask what difference the altered 'menu' of cultural resources offered by a technology such as satellite television is making to patterns of identification. My ethnographic research into the consumption of satellite TV can be seen as a modest attempt to answer that difficult question, along with several more which are to do with the dynamics of daily life in particular urban places (see Chapter 4).

I am arguing, in conclusion, that we need to reflect on our cultural associations with others – both co-present and absent – via the idea of community, taking into consideration the various channels of access which television and radio now give us to electronic landscapes. This would mean thinking carefully about our participation in day-to-day 'ceremonies' or reception rituals of the kind described by Anderson, and also about the types of imaginative 'journey' that we are being invited to go on from within the confines of the household environment.

# III  Early Radio: The Domestication of a New Media Technology

In the previous chapter, I explored the ways in which broadcasting can be thought of as an institution in everyday life – as an ordinary, taken-for-granted part of modern household cultures. My aim in this chapter is to 'deconstruct' broadcasting's relationship with the home by charting its history. One of the principal values of historical investigations is that they enable us to denaturalise our current social arrangements – showing things which we now see as given in the process of their formation – and in the following analysis, I want to return to the early years of radio in the 1920s and 1930s when it was still a new technology, asking how the medium was gradually 'domesticated' over those two decades. To borrow a phrase from Lesley Johnson (1981), early radio was involved in 'capturing time and space' in the home. The research presented here is an attempt to map its transformation from being an 'unruly guest' to becoming, symbolically at least, a 'good companion' to household members. In addition, my commentary looks to situate the emergence of 'the family audience' within a wider history of spatial and temporal divisions.

As I indicated in Chapter 1, my principal method of investigation in this research project was oral history interviews conducted with elderly people who lived in a town in the North of England. With the assistance of a community worker in the area, I gained access to 'day clubs' for the elderly and visited several of the men and women contacted there at their homes, recording numerous recollections of broadcasting's arrival in daily domestic life. My analysis of these memories tries to piece together a cultural history of early radio from the listener's point of view. Like Paul Thompson (1978), I believe that existing public accounts of the past need to be supplemented by more private, personal voices 'from below' – and my work may therefore be read as an invitation to open up alternative, audience-centred histories of broadcasting (see O'Sullivan 1991).

## An Unruly Guest in the Living Room

If broadcasting was to capture a place in the spaces and times of everyday life, then this incorporation was less than immediate. At the point of its entry into the living room during the 1920s, radio is remembered by the interviewees as the cause of some considerable disturbance to domestic routines. According to their reports, broadcasting's initial appearance in the household was marked by deep social divisions between family members. In that period, audiences for radio tended to reflect the technological novelty of the medium. Consumers concerned themselves above all with the means of reception as opposed to programme contents – and the interview material suggests it was mainly young men, caught up in the play of experimentation, who were listening to broadcast transmissions. There are many recollections of male relatives or neighbours constructing their own radio receivers at home:

Uncle Bill made our first set from a kit. Oh, he had diagrams and goodness-knows-what ... he used to get the components and piece them together. Uncle Bill was a bit of a one for hobbies.

SM: Your brother was interested in making radios from kits? Oh yes, he loved anything like that. He started building these wireless sets and he had to send away for the blueprints ... I've known him to be working on a wireless for hours and hours, he'd be telling me to clear off when I went to see how he was getting on.

As I remember, it was the young inquisitive fellas who took it up first. They'd all be messing around with these bits and pieces, just like the kids round 'ere are today with their cars, always pulling the guts out of the engine and shoving other bits back – and just like they run round for an engine part these days, so they always used to be on the look out for extra little things to improve the radio sets. It was what they'd call today 'a craze', d'you get my drift?

The other day, I was watching a programme about ... Alexander Bell, and it made me think of our old wireless set. It reminded me of when my father used to be experimenting with these radios, trying to hear a voice come through. Our first set was made from a kit ... most people had the kits.

These 'do-it-yourself' sets were popular early receivers, and articles devoted to the construction and operation of such gadgets were published in specialist periodicals. No doubt the preference for kits was partly a consequence of their relatively low cost. A home-built receiver could be bought at a vastly cheaper price than the already manufactured sets which were on sale in shops. Even so, an elementary wireless kit – purchased for around three pounds in 1923 – would still have been an expensive commodity for working-class listeners, forcing enthusiasts to acquire pieces separately and assemble their radios bit by bit. For example, a woman recalls saving money to buy the components for her husband: 'When it was his birthday or when Christmas came, I used to give him parts for his wireless, d'you see? I'd put fourpence away every week to save up and get him the bits he was after'.

The technical limitations of early radio sets made good reception a rare event: 'All you could hear was the sea, you know, like the sound of waves – but oh, there'd be such a hullabaloo if you could hear one voice, just one voice'. As historian Mark Pegg (1983: 40) has pointed out, this was 'a time when the technical problems of listening were of paramount importance, whilst programme policy or content were secondary considerations'. Indeed, he noted that three-quarters of listeners' letters sent to the BBC in the 1920s were concerned with the difficulties of getting a clear signal. Only a small minority of correspondents remarked upon the quality of programming. His observation supports a view of broadcasting as a system of communication 'devised for transmission and reception as abstract processes, with little or no definition of preceding content' (Williams 1974: 25). Radio discourses were very much in a formative stage and programme output often referred to its own mode of production. Up until 1926, for instance, technical language had a strong presence in BBC entertainment – characters appeared on air with names like 'Atmos P. Herics' and 'Oscar the Oscillator'.

So when broadcasting arrived in the private sphere, it did so in the shape of a miraculous toy – a novel gadget which husbands, fathers, brothers and uncles might playfully experiment with. Listening was a technological 'adventure'. However, early radio sets and their accessories were miracles which provided an obtrusive new addition to domestic furnishings. Paddy Scannell and David Cardiff (1991: 356) have written that, at the birth of broadcasting, 'receiving equipment looked more like something out of contemporary science fiction than a simple household object'. To pick up a signal successfully, several of the original receivers required a long aerial extension which had to be stretched to an outside mast. The following memories give an idea of just how unsightly this arrangement must have been. One speaker recalls that 'all down the backs

there'd be poles ... they'd use clothes props and brooms and things
like that, nail 'em together – as long as it was high up, you'd get a
better sound'. A second interviewee says: 'Oh, it was something out
of the ordinary in them days, having this box in the living room ...
there was a square piece of wood and on it was all these wires'. 'You
had', she continues, 'to have a big pole at the bottom of the yard
with a wire coming right in ... all along the living room wall'.
Evidently, the wireless did not always live up to its name.

A particular sort of set, which was powered by heavy wet-cell
'accumulators', constituted a double hazard – to the furniture it
rested on and to the family member who took the batteries to be
recharged, usually at the local bicycle shop:

> I remember once when a battery leaked. It was on the dresser,
> and it leaked all over the carpet and left a big white patch. My
> mother was furious.

> We used to have the radio on the sideboard in the living room.
> My mother used to be going mad ... in case it took the polish
> off ... my mother didn't like it on there, she was always
> polishing and that ... I don't think she was as interested in the
> radio as my dad.

> I remember when I had to take those batteries to be recharged.
> I was only a young girl. I used to take this glass-looking
> battery to the cycle shop. My mother used to tell me to keep it
> away from my clothes because there was acid in them, and I
> used to walk up the street very gingerly with it.

> You had to be careful how you carried 'em. If you dropped
> one, you'd run like hell.

Corrosive acid, coupled with the ungainly mechanical appearance
of the original sets, meant that radio's location in some households
remained uncertain. Here, for example, is a description which
illustrates precisely this 'transitional' stage in the domestic history
of broadcasting: 'We used to put it away in either the cupboard or
the pantry when we weren't using it. We only brought it out when
we wanted it on. It wasn't like television, stood in the corner, it was
brought out'.

It is also important to bear in mind that, for the majority of
people who came into contact with radio in the 1920s, listening to
the wireless was not a shared experience. Initially, because many of
the sets lacked speakers to amplify incoming messages, broadcasts
were commonly heard over headphones. The apparatus prescribed

individual reception and its single listener typically seems to have been male. In fact, on occasion, wives and daughters could be actively excluded from or silenced by radio consumption practices – leading women to feel frustrated with the situation:

> Only one of us could listen-in and that was my husband. The rest of us were sat like mummies. We used to row over it when we were courting. I used to say, 'I'm not coming down to your house just to sit around like a stupid fool'. He always had these earphones on, messing with the wire, trying to get different stations. He'd be saying, 'I've got another one', but of course we could never hear it – you could never get those earphones off his head.

> I had to sit with my arms folded while he was fiddling with his crystal. If you even moved, he'd be going 'shush shush', you know. You couldn't even go and peel potatoes, because he used to say he could hear the sound of the droppings in the sink above what was coming through the headphones.

> SM: Did the set have headphones?
> Oh yes, only one person could listen at a time.
> SM: Who had first choice?
> My father, of course. I remember he used to listen to the news with the earphones on. I don't think we ever heard the news, my father always got the earphones. Well, he was in charge, you see – what he said went.

> My father, he was a bit short tempered – and he'd be saying, 'Would you bloody well shut up', threatening us if we opened our mouths. Oh God, we daren't move when my father had that wireless on. None of us dared move a muscle.

There is clearly a comparison to be drawn between these accounts of radio in day-to-day life during the 1920s and the ethnographic research on family TV viewing which was discussed in Chapter 2. In analysing the operation of power in domestic cultures, David Morley (1986) argued that the contemporary remote control device used to switch channels is appropriated by men as a sign of patriarchal authority, referring to the object as a twentieth-century descendant of the 'medieval mace'. Perhaps the earphones worn by early radio enthusiasts might then be read as a kind of crown, with similar connotations of power and control.

At any rate, the oral history interviews which I recorded all point to the conclusion that – in this phase of broadcasting's development

– radio had quite different meanings across gender divisions and those varied interpretations were a focus of friction in households. For men, radio was a 'craze' or a 'toy', yet women perceived it as an ugly box and an imposed silence. The masculine pleasures of reception were grounded in the technical apparatus itself. Women were often literally excluded from listening, but their social relationship to the wireless was about to go through a transformation which would symbolically reposition them at the heart of the intended audience, and this transformation proved pivotal to radio's capturing of time and space in the home. It also contributed to an increasing 'privatisation' of cultural pursuits in modern society. My study now identifies three interconnected shifts that took place in the 1930s in the period leading up to the Second World War. First, the mechanical operation and aesthetic style of the radio set changed dramatically, turning it into a source of shared entertainment and a fashionable piece of living-room furniture. Secondly, there was the introduction of broadcast discourses which addressed their listening audience as the family, while specifically seeking to 'interpellate' (Althusser 1984) mothers as the feminine monitors of domestic life. Finally, broadcasters began to order their programme output into fixed schedules that revolved around the rhythm of daily routines and especially the imagined activities of the housewife.

## Changes in the Operation and Style of the Set

By 1932, sets run off mains electricity were already being sold in greater numbers than the early contraptions described above. Although not all households would have had access to an electricity supply, radio manufacturers encouraged consumers to get 'mains minded' (see Scannell and Cardiff 1991). The pre-manufactured mains set, which remained expensive at five or six guineas for even the cheapest of models, was nevertheless dropping in price – and this newer wireless equipment made its entry into the domestic sphere at a moment when many homes were becoming more comfortable places to live in. A crucial advance in the technical apparatus was the ability these machines had to separate one incoming signal from another and to amplify sound through a small loudspeaker. So basic problems with interference on reception decreased as a result of improved tuning, while listeners were no longer reliant on headphones to hear broadcast material. The days of the boffin, experimenting with set construction, were coming to an end. Programme content was fast gaining in importance for audiences, over and above the actual means of communication and the pleasures of technological 'tinkering'.

Even before this change, there is evidence in the oral history data I gathered that some consumers had started to modify their kit-built gadgets for group listening of a primitive sort. Consider these two stories which were told to me by interviewees:

> There was a basin my brother would put on the living room table, and then he'd get the earphones. There'd be my other brothers and my sister crowding round this basin and listening to the sound coming out.
>
> *SM*: Sorry ... what exactly was this basin doing?
>
> Well, my brother used to put the earphones in the basin and the sound was amplified by it. I can vividly remember the family crowding round and listening with their ears all close up to this basin on the table. The sound must only have been very faint, but it meant that more than one person could listen at a time.

> I'd put the earphones on, and then anything my wife wanted to listen to, I'd turn one earphone outwards and she used to lean her head against mine − put her ear to it. Then we both used to listen together.

Soon after, though, such bodily contortions could be avoided − as an amplification system enabled household groups to sit back and concentrate on the programmes being transmitted. Styles of wireless design altered during this period, too, with radio becoming a far less obtrusive part of the furniture − blending in with the fixtures and fittings of the living room. Pegg (1983: 56) explained how manufacturers 'decided to give designers their head ... exploiting the flexibility of ... materials like Bakelite'. In advertisements, Murphy claimed its sets possessed 'a quiet dignified style in harmony with any furniture'. Meanwhile, rival company Pye was proudly announcing in its publicity material that 'the survival of the experimental era in the outward appearance of radio belongs to a chapter ... closed by the introduction of the Pye "Cambridge Radio"'. 'Realistic entertainment and artistic beauty', it boasted, 'have long since overshadowed the miracle of radio in the minds of listeners'. Similarly, a BBC *Radio Times* editorial from 1931 heralded the changes by stating how 'the novelty of 1922 has become ... day-to-day routine' − and shortly afterwards, the well-known broadcasting critic Filson Young (1933) was able to call the medium 'that inexhaustible familiar'. The wireless phenomenon was passing from the miraculous to the taken-for-granted.

Its shifting cultural status and domestic significance are well demonstrated in this particular memory, in which a mains set was purchased by a man as a special present for his spouse back in the late 1930s: 'I can remember it now, a black Ebonite affair. That cost me four guineas. I carried it all the way home for her from the wireless shop'. In the interview extract below, a married couple give detailed descriptions of the position occupied by the object in their parents' houses shortly before the war:

> *Husband*: There was the fireplace, and next to the fireplace was my father's chair, and behind that there was a bit of a recess near the chimney breast. Aye, that's right. On the other side, there was a cupboard next to the window and near to this cupboard was another recess, and in that recess there was a shelf with glassware and ornaments on – you know, pots and china and that. Well, just underneath, there was a ledge for the wireless to go on.
>
> *Wife*: Now I remember our living room was different to yours. We had a cupboard next to the window, and where we used to keep the coal, that was next to it. Then there was a door next to the coalplace which led to the hallway and right opposite there was the door leading to the kitchen. We had a trolley in the corner next to that door, and the wireless was on top of there ... Well, it was a fixture, wasn't it?

Here, the accepted place of radio in the 'micro-geography' of the home is carefully recalled.

Social surveys carried out at the end of the 1930s – by Hilda Jennings and Winnifred Gill (1939) in Bristol, and by Seebohm Rowntree (1941) in York – made the case that broadcasting had significantly increased the attractiveness of the household as a dwelling place and as a site of leisure. Both of these surveys drew a rather exaggerated comparison between a previous time when – in the words of Jennings and Gill (1939: 21) – 'the street and the public house offered the main scope for recreation', and a new situation in which the cultural activities of working-class people were rapidly 'retreating' into the private sphere. From the authors' middle-class viewpoint, this withdrawal to interior space was seen as a move in the right direction. What Rowntree referred to as the 'cosy companionship' of radio in the home was contrasted with a far more threatening image of 'the unruly mob' that had long haunted the bourgeois imagination.

Judging from the following remarks made by two female interviewees, this same contrast was finding expression in elements

of the popular imagination as well. One of them talks enthus-
iastically about her enjoyment of dance band music, but when
asked whether she used to go out dancing, the woman replies: 'Oh
no, you see my father wouldn't let me ... he thought these dance
halls were dens of iniquity, so there would've been trouble if I'd
ever gone there'. However, she continues, 'I used to listen to jazz on
the radio at home ... well that was different'. Another says of her
father: 'He liked us under his nose ... we were encouraged to stay in
... A lot of people were quite content to sit in, in fact my father had
beer in at the weekend rather than going to the pub'. Of course,
while these speakers remember listening to radio within the
confines of the domestic, many of their contemporaries in the 1930s
would indeed have been out at the dance hall or pub. There was no
overnight disappearance of public working-class culture. Still, the
stories which they tell – together with the accounts given by
Jennings, Gill and Rowntree – do indicate a shifting relationship
between private and public settings of modern social life, and they
also identify broadcasting as an important contribution to the shift.

At the end of the inter-war decades, the technology and output
of radio may have added to the home's appeal – but I want to stress
that the social and spatial arrangements of the household served, in
turn, to regulate the ways in which broadcasting could be utilised
by its listeners. The sorts of house where my interviewees were
living in the 1920s and 1930s are typical of the terraced properties
built extensively by speculative firms from the start of the twentieth century. A front room, the 'parlour', was usually reserved for
Sundays and special occasions – and the living room at the rear
would either double as, or be directly connected to, a back kitchen.
This was the place where meals were cooked and eaten, and where
families might often gather together in the evening. The internal
geography of the home provided certain frameworks for household
practices (see Foucault 1980). It 'prescribed' a model of domesticity,
helping to establish an identity and morality for the family group.

## Family Listening and the Mother as Monitor

Radio's evolving discourses came to be targeted at the family
audience – either at the household group as a whole or, in particular
scheduled slots, at selected family members. Its modes of address
sought to reinforce the prescribed model of domestic relations which
I pointed to at the close of my previous section. Broadcasting thought
of itself as 'one of the family', with the task of supplying the kind of
cosy companionship that Rowntree spoke of in his survey. This role

was perhaps best symbolised by a programme like *Children's Hour*, in which radio 'aunts' and 'uncles' kept the youngsters amused while Mum prepared the evening meal. Wireless presenters here played the part of extended kin, lending a hand with childcare at a busy time of the day. More generally, the 1930s saw the development of what are now very familiar evening entertainment formats. Quiz shows, serials and variety performances were essential in constructing the shared 'pleasures of the hearth' (Frith 1983).

Indeed, the image of the fireside was commonplace in broadcasting literature of the period. A winter issue of the *Radio Times* in 1935 declared: 'To close the door behind you, with the curtains drawn against the rain, and the fire glowing in the hearth – that is one of the real pleasures of life'. 'And it is when you are settled by your own fireside', continued the copy, 'that you most appreciate the entertainment that broadcasting can bring'. Scannell and Cardiff (1982: 168) note how the home was seen as 'an enclave, a retreat burrowed deeply away from the pressures of urban living'. This is a striking expression of what the French philosopher Gaston Bachelard (1969) has called the 'dialectics of outside and inside'. The hearth and the wireless were represented together as a focus of interior space and family pleasure. Of course, what the *Radio Times* offered was an idealised picture of the household in harmony – and actual living rooms were presumably less cosy, more conflict-ridden places – yet its preferred image was still a remarkable move away from the earlier significance of radio as a 'toy for the boys'.

Previously excluded from the audience, housewives and mothers were in many ways central to broadcasting's new 'hailing' of the family. Daytime radio features addressed the woman as monitor of the private sphere, issuing her with information on childcare techniques or advice on home management. Jennings and Gill (1939: 17) wrote about the everyday reception of these programmes:

> Doctors' talks on Friday mornings were said to be helpful practically, especially by mothers of small children, many of whom ... have become more open minded and ready to seek advice as a result of the teaching of Mothercraft in the infant welfare centres. Some women said they found talks on laundry work and other branches of household management useful ... Their whole attitude to housekeeping and motherhood is undergoing modification in the direction of increased knowledge, control and dignity.

Health of family members was equated in these discourses with the general 'health of the nation'. The welfare of individual bodies and that of the whole 'social body' were quite explicitly connected. So, for instance, in 1931 the *Listener* magazine stated: 'Our bad food habits are responsible for impairing our national capacity for work and output ... The loss of the nation's time through sickness disablement in industry now averages no less than a fortnight per head per year'. A pamphlet for mothers, *Choosing the Right Food*, was published by the BBC – in which doctors advised on the planning of a well-balanced diet from basic foodstuffs. The Minister of Health delivered a radio talk entitled 'Motherhood and a Fitter Nation', encouraging women to forge closer links with the doctor, the clinic and the hospital – whilst in 1934, a series of lectures was transmitted on topics like 'Strong Bones and Good Muscles', 'Teeth and their Troubles' and 'Colds, Tonsils and Adenoids'.

A possible, Foucauldian interpretation of this 'explosion of discourse' around the management of domestic life is that broadcasting was caught up in a complex reorientation of the operations of power in modern society. From such a perspective, 'government through the family' (Donzelot 1980) – exercised from within – replaced a straightforward government of families from above, with the mother being singled out as the main point of support in efforts to reform the household group. She could be understood as the state's 'delegate', responsible for the physical and moral welfare of her husband and children. In venturing this explanation of the situation, I am well aware of the potential confusion which may arise from any proposal that housewives were 'invested with power' in the process – given the arguments made elsewhere in my book about gender inequalities in domestic cultures. It is necessary to remember that women's empowerment here was always limited to specific areas of social activity – and, furthermore, it was certainly not in their material or political interests to be positioned in the monitorial role (see Barrett and McIntosh 1982).

## Scheduling and the Rhythm of Daily Routines

Up to now, I have focused on radio's capturing of space in the home and on the ways in which broadcasters addressed audiences located in household settings, but it was only with the allied capture of family time that the domestication of the technology – its integration into day-to-day life – was completed. Back in the experimental era of broadcasting, there had been a deliberate avoidance of continuity and regularity in the organisation of programming (Scannell 1988). Periods of silence were left in the gaps between individual programmes and the same feature might return at a different moment each week. The purpose of these disruptions was to encourage selective and attentive consumption, rather than allowing listeners to slip into regular patterns of everyday use. However, with the increasing success of foreign competitors like Radio Luxembourg in delivering popular forms of output at times which viewers could rely upon, there was a gradual move by the BBC during the 1930s towards more predictable scheduling that 'chimed in' with existing domestic rituals. Radio in Britain began to fit itself into the repetitive rhythm of quotidian culture.

It was the imagined daily routine of the mother which provided a basis for the broadcasters' new programming plans. Her supposed round of household activities was adopted as a general guide to the changing shape of audiences throughout the day, as schedulers tried to take account of when different people would be listening. Below, one of my interviewees recalls precisely how the resulting schedules came to be interwoven with mundane practices of housework and child rearing. He also indicates overlaps with the man's work and leisure, with the youngsters' school and bedtimes, and with the whole family's mealtime and evening relaxation:

I remember *Housewives' Choice* for women who were at home in the morning. It started about nine o'clock, and housewives used to write off and ask for a record. Oh, and *Listen with Mother* at lunchtime, for women with young children at home. There was a children's programme on late afternoon for when the older ones came in from school, and then there was the news on at the same time every night – I always used to listen to that when I came in from work, during the evening meal. Then later, there'd be music or shows or stories – maybe a quiz – and I used to have favourite programmes on different nights of the week. I remember there used to be a programme called *Monday Night at Seven* ... of course, with everyone being in early evening, they used to put things on that kids could listen to as well ... something for all the family.

Johnson (1981) argued that early Australian radio promoted itself as the constant companion of housewives, and the BBC developed similar scheduling strategies. Still, it is important to highlight instances in which women did not – or were unable to – accept the 'friendly' offer of company. For example, when asked whether she had listened during the day, a woman replies: 'I never had time. There were too many jobs to do, what with baking and washing and all that'. In this case, part of the problem seems to have been the positioning of the set. Her memory is that 'the radio was in the parlour, whereas I'd be in the back most of the time'. Keeping the wireless in the front room of the house appears to have signified a 'Sunday best' attitude to broadcasting, as compared with the usual placing of the object in the rear living room, where it offered a background accompaniment to routine tasks.

A crucial point in the schedules was the transition from daytime broadcasting to evening listening, often the moment of the family meal. On this matter, Pegg (1983: 143) referred to the words of another social survey from the late 1930s entitled *The People's Food*, which noted that 'the hour of the tea-time meal is even more important to wireless broadcasters than breakfast and lunch'. The authors of the report warned: 'a programme of special interest to housewives will not secure its maximum listening public if it clashes with the preparation of tea or the washing up'. Subsequent evening entertainment slowly started to fall into regular nightly and weekly patterns – by 1937, there were already forty fixed slots in BBC output after six o'clock (see Scannell and Cardiff 1982) – but repetitive scheduling was not fully established until the 1940s. In fact, of the programmes named above in the interview extract, only *Monday Night at Seven* does not date from the Second World War or later. There is evidently a compression of 'linear time' in the speaker's account, with the rhythms of 'cyclical time' having left a much stronger trace in the memory.

To appreciate this growing concern among broadcasters with temporal segmentation and repetition, it is necessary to understand something about the pre-existing arrangements into which radio schedules fitted. Just as broadcasting was inserted into an histori- cally specific organisation of space, so it entered particular social divisions of time. In an essay on capitalist work-discipline, Edward Thompson (1967) proposed that the temporal structuring of every- day life in modern society has its roots in the regulation of a large industrial labour force. His research charts a 'general diffusion of clocks and watches ... occurring at the exact moment when the industrial revolution demanded a greater synchronisation of labour' (Thompson 1967: 69). Similarly, Anthony Giddens (1981) wondered whether the clock – rather than the steam engine – ought to be regarded as the epitome of industrialisation. He has discussed how 'the "working day", calculated by worker and employee alike in terms of commodified time, became central to the worker's experience' (Giddens 1981: 137). Equally significant was the separation of home from workplace and the cultural con- struction of so-called 'free time' outside the factory. With this break came the emergence of new temporal markers such as 'the weekend', periods which were also of particular interest to broadcasters.

Radio helped to bring precise temporal measurement into the private sphere. It domesticated standard national time. Of course, there were clocks in many households long before the wireless arrived – but only with the development of broadcasting did synchronised, nationwide signals get relayed directly and simultaneously into millions of living rooms. Young (1933: 252) pointed out that: 'The broadcasting of time, which is one of the most commonplace and regular features of the daily programme, is also, rightly considered, one of the strangest of the new things that the harnessing of the ether has brought us'. The broadcast sound of the Big Ben clock tower at Westminster was celebrated in this 1930s poem from the *Radio Times*: 'Time for the time signal – speak, Big Ben; / Boom out the time to children and men; / Over Great Britain's listening isles; / Send your voice ringing for miles upon miles'. It is difficult to gauge just how compliant listeners were to these imposed temporal structures, although a remarkable character does appear in the interview transcripts:

> My father, everybody used to keep time by him. If they saw him walking down the street to work in a morning, they knew it was a certain time, to the minute. He was never late and never early either. He wound his clocks up at the same time every night ... he used to listen to the radio for the time checks ... he'd get home from work, and each and every night he'd put the news on, regular as anything.

This sort of routinised behaviour can be compared with what Benedict Anderson (1983) termed the ceremonial act of reading a national newspaper each morning. Opening the pages of the daily paper – and switching on the news bulletin each evening to hear the chimes of Big Ben – are practices which enable people to imagine themselves as part of a social collectivity that shares in the same anonymous, simultaneously performed rituals.

BBC radio sought to build a sense of collective national identity by creating an annual calendar of public events and occasions alongside the little ceremonies of everyday consumption. According to Cardiff and Scannell (1987: 159–60): 'Special anniversary programmes marked the great religious festivals, Christmas and Easter ... included in the same round were ... days of solemn remembrance and national pride such as Armistice Day or Empire Day ... sporting occasions, the FA Cup Final and the Boat Race'. In addition, broadcasting in Britain over the years has consistently attempted to bring the monarchy into closer contact with ordinary people – providing coverage of coronations, jubilees and royal weddings, as well as instituting annual events of its own such as the monarch's Christmas Day speech. Starting in the early 1930s, the king sent the best wishes of his family to the assembled listeners at home, symbolically binding together a united 'national family'.

However, I would contend that social historians like Cardiff and Scannell – who have done exemplary work on broadcasting as an institution of cultural production – are in danger of implicitly assuming audiences to have identified unproblematically with those forms of output. Whilst all of the respondents in my oral history research had listened to most of the broadcasts mentioned here by Cardiff and Scannell, by no means all were willing to recognise themselves straightforwardly as patriotic national subjects. For instance, there are memories of some families poking fun at the king's voice during his Christmas Day speech. Another interesting example from the interview data is a story about young men in the town going round on the morning of the Boat Race with Oxford or Cambridge rosettes pinned to their jacket lapels. On the face of it, this account seems to indicate popular acceptance of a university rowing match held in London as part of a shared national calendar – whereas, in fact, the enthusiasm had to do chiefly with opportunities which the contest afforded for betting. Imagined communities and collective identities need to be seen as a product of articulations between the public and the private, and they are not always successfully forged. In Chapter 4, amongst other things, I try to show how qualitative research on media consumers can aid in the examination of these interdiscursive processes.

# IV Satellite Television: Audiences and Articulations

As in Chapter 3, I am concerned here with the arrival of a new media technology in everyday life, but my focus in the present chapter is on a much later period in the history of broadcasting in Britain – the era of so-called deregulation and, in particular, the coming of direct broadcast satellite TV. Reporting on ethnographic research carried out in domestic and neighbourhood settings, I reflect on the cultural significance of satellite television as an object of consumption. My analysis seeks to identify the technology's varied uses and meanings for different audiences. In the course of this qualitative investigation, I spoke with members of eighteen households in which a dish had recently been acquired. Their homes were all situated in the same South Wales city, and my sample was drawn from three separate residential areas in that urban locale, with six houses visited in each district.

This research should be seen as a study of 'articulations', in two overlapping senses of the term defined for us by Stuart Hall (1986a) in his work on discourse and power. 'The word "articulation" ... has a nice double meaning', he notes, 'because "articulate" means to utter, to speak ... It carries that sense of language-ing, of expressing ... But we also speak of an "articulated" lorry ... where the front (cab) and back (trailer) can, but need not necessarily, be connected to one another' (Hall 1986a: 53). Expressions and connections are absolutely central to the following analysis. I offer an interpretation of people's talk about their relationships with technologies, and with each other, in consumer cultures – listening to how identities or distinctions are actively 'voiced' there, in both the talk and the social relationships. In doing so, it is also my intention to highlight the ways in which an object like satellite TV gets 'embedded' in the practices and structures of households, neighbourhoods and broader cultural communities. We need to locate points of connection, provisional linkages, between the artefact and its social contexts (see Slack 1989).

## Background to the Study

At the time I conducted my research, direct broadcast satellite television was still very much in its infancy. Although a limited satellite broadcasting service had been available in Britain since the early 1980s, mainly via cable TV networks, it was not until the latter part of the decade that more widespread direct-to-home transmission took off. Domestic consumers could now purchase or rent a small dish-shaped aerial and accompanying receiver unit at relatively low cost. For example, the most common household dish – Amstrad's Fidelity model – was being sold in the high street during 1990 at just under two hundred pounds. This was considerably cheaper than any of the large motorised dishes previously bought by enthusiasts. Following the launch of the first Astra telecommunications satellite, which planted a transnational 'footprint' across Western Europe, Rupert Murdoch's Sky Television company began broadcasting in February 1989. A rival enterprise, British Satellite Broadcasting, went on air shortly afterwards – marketing its distinctive 'squarial' system to potential viewers – but by November 1990, the two organisations had merged in what was generally perceived in the media industry as a takeover of BSB by Sky. Looking at the broader economic and political background to these events, we can see the rise of 'popular capitalism' in Britain under a Thatcherite Conservative administration which committed itself to deregulating broadcasting. The principles of commercial competition and consumer choice were fundamental to government policies of the day, and also to the corporate and advertising strategies of satellite television companies.

Another significant feature of the promotional discourses surrounding this communication technology was the emphasis put on its futuristic, 'space-age' connotations. Initially, advertisements produced by broadcasters and hardware manufacturers drew on the codes of science fiction – for instance, incorporating images of 'flying saucer' dishes on a cratered moonscape – while photographs of satellite rocket launches appeared in specialist consumer magazines. A clear symbolic opposition is set up for us here, between the old-established 'terrestrial' TV services and the 'whole new world of television' being beamed straight into living rooms from an extra-terrestrial source.

In terms of the form and content of broadcast output – the technology's software, so to speak – satellite TV's arrival marked an important shift in the organisation of programme schedules, and in the number of channels that were available to those who possessed a dish. Largely dispensing with the ethos of mixed programming which is dominant in national terrestrial television, satellite broadcasters prefer to deliver thematic packages. The principle of 'internal pluralism', variety of output from a single station, gives way to that of 'external pluralism' – where there is a far stronger branding of content within a multi-channel viewing environment (Collins 1990a). So news, sport, films and pop music are kept separate from each other and given their own independent schedules. Channels often target specific audience groupings or market segments. As well as the diverse range of programme materials in English, there are several European foreign-language channels transmitted via Astra. If this diversity brought increased competition and choice, it also heralded a heated debate about 'quality' in broadcasting (see Mulgan 1990), or what critics of satellite TV usually saw as a lack of it. Partly because of Murdoch's ownership of the *Sun* newspaper, Sky became known to its detractors as 'tabloid television'.

The interpretative descriptions which I present below are intended to contribute to our understanding of how such changes were experienced by audiences at the moment of consumption and use. Responses to, or consequences of, technological innovation – and related shifts in media policy, promotional culture and programme supply – cannot be assumed at an abstract level of analysis. They require close examination at the point of connection with concrete day-to-day situations that social subjects inhabit and make meaningful. Ethnographic research of this sort, then, is designed to gain an 'insider's view' of the cultural worlds of domestic consumers. In the case of my own study, the aim was to document a crucial period in broadcasting's evolution from the perspectives of household members who are city dwellers.

My three urban neighbourhoods were chosen because they represent different kinds of housing stock located at varying distances from a city centre, and they could reasonably be expected to deliver research subjects with a spread of socio-economic and cultural positions. To begin with, I spent lengthy periods walking around these areas, getting a feel for the character of the district and noting down specific addresses where satellite dishes had appeared. Letters were written to the residents at those addresses, briefly outlining my project and informing them that I would be calling to request an informal interview in the domestic context – which, if they were willing to participate, would be arranged at their convenience for a later date. In order to obtain a total of eighteen households, I approached just over twice this number.

Given that the main criteria for approaching a home were to do with its geographical location and the possession of a visible dish, my sample contains no uniform household type. So unlike David Morley (1986), I do not focus exclusively on 'conventional' nuclear families. Instead, this is merely one living arrangement found amongst others. Neither was it always possible to interview all the members of a household, as Morley had done in his work on family TV viewing. On occasion, they could not be assembled together at a single convenient time, or else certain individuals were 'nominated' to speak about satellite television for the whole group. There are obvious problems associated with such a nomination process, particularly when it is only the most powerful and committed voices which get heard – but this can, in turn, be incorporated as part of the data on a domestic culture.

Interviews were typically relaxed in manner and conversational in tone – lasting up to two hours – and whilst I kept a mental checklist of key topics to be covered, informants were allowed the space to pursue issues which they perceived to be relevant. They were encouraged to speak from experience and to relate episodes from their daily lives. My style of questioning was chiefly open-ended, tailored to producing narrative responses rather than short answers. For example, I started each interview by asking respondents to tell me the story of how they came to get satellite TV in their home. This frequently provoked a lengthy account of who initially had the idea of installing a dish and why, or maybe an argument between family members over whether it was the right decision to purchase the equipment. Usually, our discussions were recorded in the living room where the principal television set was being watched – although, when appropriate, I was shown into other rooms too. Some observation was therefore possible during visits, and notes were made immediately afterwards on a household's interior layout, decorative mode and interpersonal dynamics.

## Neighbourhood A: Edwardian Bay-Fronted

In the first of three sections which report on the findings of my empirical research, I want to concentrate on data from a neighbourhood that lies approximately five kilometres from the centre of the city. This particular district is made up of privately owned properties which were built at the beginning of the twentieth century, a collection of large, bay-fronted Edwardian terraces and detached houses. Passing right through it is a small park with trees and a stream, surrounded by ornate antique railings. Estate agents refer to the 'authentic' historical character of the area, and while some of the road names echo those of English stately homes, others recall famous military battles overseas. Neighbourhood A has a mixed population of skilled blue-collar workers and middle-class professionals, and in certain respects it is comparable with a community in the North-West of England observed by sociologist Derek Wynne (1990). He sought to contrast the lifestyles and leisure patterns of housing estate residents with very different types of cultural capital at their disposal. His fieldwork highlighted the frictions between them over matters of taste. Similar clashes of disposition and taste, in the district described here, give rise to anxieties about satellite TV that are frequently expressed in my conversational interviews with 'dish-erectors'.

A distinguishing feature of the neighbourhood I am analysing is its age. Whereas Wynne's ethnography was conducted out of town on a modern estate, the homes featured in this section are located in a suburb which – for reasons outlined in the paragraph above – has strong connotations of 'heritage'. In these circumstances, the arrival of a new media technology – with its futuristic dish aerial on open display – results in a curious collision of aesthetic and cultural codes. Charlotte Brunsdon (1991), in her review of newspaper reports on controversies over the siting of dishes, noted how tensions tend to surface when the objects are installed on old buildings considered to have architectural merit. Discourses of 'innovation' and 'conservation' confront each other head on, exerting pressure in opposite directions, and it is precisely that contradiction between senses of the modern and the traditional which runs through much of my subsequent commentary. Such a conflict, I will argue, is not confined to antagonisms at the level of the residential area. It can get 'gridded' in complex and shifting ways on to social divisions of gender and generation in domestic life, and may also help to constitute broader feelings of collective identity.

### The Gibsons

Let me start to unpack my initial remarks on this neighbourhood by looking in some detail at one of the homes I visited there. A family I shall call the Gibsons – the names of all households participating in the study have been changed – live in an old property that had previously belonged to a well-known family of solicitors in the city, and their aerial is a rarely seen Cambridge model. There is a striking divergence of tastes and competences here between Mr Gibson and his nineteen-year-old son. The father takes great pleasure in talking about the 'character' and heritage value of the building they own. He is currently restoring an original antique fireplace, which he discovered hidden behind a plasterboard wall, and has plans to strip and varnish a built-in wooden dresser in the back dining room. Mr Gibson is extremely anxious about the dish's appearance on their housefront. It was the son, Tony, who wanted satellite television. Since he left school three years ago and gained his own independent source of income as a shiftworker in a bakery, Tony has chosen to buy a range of the latest media technologies. These commodities adorn his attic bedroom, described to me by his father as 'a conglomeration of electronics'.

Tony's room at the top of the house is separated from the main living area by a narrow staircase and landing. He is intensely proud of this space and the artefacts that are arranged inside it, regarding the attic as a place into which he can retreat, and as a symbol of independence from the rest of his family. Showing me the bedroom, Tony explains:

> I'm the only one who knows how to use any of my electrical equipment. Nobody else comes in my room, I think of it as my space … Up here I can watch anything I want, read, sleep, think about life, listen to music … As soon as I go into my room it's like I'm on another planet.

Gathered around his TV set, there is a remarkable 'entourage' (Leal 1990) of technical goods, decorative images and objects. Two video recorders, a hi-fi system and the satellite receiver are all stacked on shelves underneath the television. They have been wired together so that the sound comes out of four Dolby Surround speakers mounted on brackets in each corner of the room. According to Mr Gibson, 'it's like a disco in there … if he turned the volume up any more, it'd blow the whole roof off'. Tony has moved his bed to a central point between these speakers, and five different remote control devices rest on top of the duvet cover. This cover, like the alarm clock on his bedside table which wakes him in time for the shiftwork, is decorated with characters from *The Simpsons* – an American cartoon show that goes out on Sky One. On the walls are posters of sports cars, while neatly ordered piles of video tapes and compact discs lie on the floor. His viewing preferences are for science fiction and horror – recording several films off the Sky Movies channel – and he collects tapes about the making of films as well, notably those concerned with special effects or stunts.

It is possible, I believe, to read these assembled goods as signs of a struggle to fashion some limited degree of autonomy in the face of parental authority. He does not have a home of his own, still relying on parents for accommodation, but Tony's job at the bakery enables him to save up and purchase things – items which are treasured precisely because they provide a statement of personal identity. Of course, that identity takes shape under conditions not entirely of his own choosing. He is, as the post-structuralists might say, constituted as a subject only as a consequence of being subjected to the 'symbolic order' of culture. Tony inhabits a specifically masculine world of gadgets, fast cars and sci-fi fantasies, a world of meaning which he shares with many of his friends and fellow male workers.

However, my suggestion would be that we adopt a more 'culturalist' (see Hall 1986b) perspective on Tony's situation – one which recognises a measure of human agency, and enables us to understand the tensions between social reproduction and resistance. For this teenager in this immediate context, satellite TV is part of a 'constellation' of technologies and practices which supplies him with the resources to express difference and establish competence. It is important to appreciate his 'symbolic creativity' (Willis 1990) in circumstances of material and ideological constraint. Tellingly, his father confesses complete incompetence when it comes to operating the machinery in Tony's bedroom: 'He knows where everything is, but I don't ... I remember glancing over at it, the electronics and wiring, and just one look was enough for me'.

Mr Gibson's interest in restoring antique furnishings and fittings has grown considerably over the period since satellite television entered their home. This heightened investment in 'the old' is presumably a direct response to his son's passion for 'the new'. Tony makes a partial bid for independence. His father, meanwhile, defines a clearly contrasting field of knowledge and skills. The generational division is evident, although there remains an intriguing exception to that general rule. Mrs Gibson's taste for pop music from the 1960s has been 'inherited' by Tony – who started to borrow her scratched and dusty LP records when he was still at school – and those same recordings have now been bought on CD, forming a large part of the musical library in his attic room. Perhaps the raiding of styles from a previous era is not so surprising, given the trend in contemporary youth culture which Dick Hebdige (1988) has termed 'retro-chic', but it does add a further twist to oppositions between the traditional and the modern in the Gibson household.

The story of how their external aerial got selected is a revealing account of conflict and compromise. In this instance, installing satellite TV was a potential cause of embarrassment for Mr Gibson, given the 'tone' of the neighbourhood that they live in. Realising the technical impracticalities of siting at the rear of the house, as dishes must be aligned at a particular angle to the sky in order to pick up transmissions, Tony had to enter into a protracted debate with his father about the aesthetics of display. His father's comments on the circular Amstrad Fidelity dishes are decidedly uncomplimentary. Mr Gibson calls them 'frying pans', and says:

> They look completely out of place on houses like this, old houses with character ... I didn't want an unsightly thing hovering up there. If it was just a prefabricated sort of house, then sure, I wouldn't mind – but as we've got bay windows and all the stonework at the front, I wasn't going to have something that wouldn't blend in ... wouldn't retain the character of the area.

After consulting consumer guide magazines which were obtained from the local newsagents, Tony eventually managed to convince him of the Cambridge system's unobtrusive qualities. The name itself connotes a higher-status commodity, offering associations of 'education' and heritage, and its aerial is a rectangular stone-coloured block with a round hollow 'carved' into it – rather than the usual white or black mesh disc design. Even Mr Gibson admits that 'it's compact and looks neater on the side of houses ... there's many a person'll pass and not notice you've got it'. I return to this theme of invisibility later in the section.

My final remarks on the Gibsons provide a convenient link with the next household 'portrait' which I sketch – and they concern this family's identifications, through television, with larger national or transnational communities. It might be argued that small-scale ethnographic research of the sort reported here is an inappropriate means of investigating the construction of collective identities. Much of the existing work on this theme in media and cultural studies has taken public representations and narratives as a starting point for analysis, rather than trying to explore the sentiments of actual social subjects in the private domain. However, as Michael Billig (1992) has succeeded in demonstrating – in his book on attitudes to the British monarchy – conversational interviews with families can be of the utmost relevance for examining discourses of community as they are articulated 'on the ground' in routine domestic contexts.

Talk about TV – in both its terrestrial and satellite varieties – may be able to deliver similar, if fleeting, insights into these processes of identification. For example, in the case of the Gibsons there is an interesting distinction which is made between different image spaces or territories of transmission. Tony's positive feelings about the Astra broadcasts – he tunes in to continental stations like

RTL Plus or Pro 7, as well as the Sky channels and MTV Europe – are intimately related to his dismissal of established terrestrial programming as traditional, boring and old fashioned. In fact, he labels this negatively as 'British television'. His parents use precisely the same label themselves, but for them its value is reversed. They prefer to watch BBC and ITV in the living room downstairs.

## The Harveys

For the Harveys, a family living nearby, there are further interesting connections being forged between everyday experience and the new 'spaces of identity' made available by satellite TV. Sam and Liz Harvey are in their late twenties and have three children aged five years, four years and six months. They moved to South Wales from the Midlands region of England, where Sam had studied for his polytechnic degree in electronic engineering. Liz works as a housewife and her husband is now self-employed, having resigned from a salaried job to start up a small business designing and manufacturing computer robotics equipment for export. This married couple perceive the satellite technology to be giving them an expanded range of viewing choices – although Sam gets to exercise that choice more than Liz – and, significantly, he speaks about the 'larger feel' created by a type of television transmission which transcends the boundaries of narrowly British broadcasting.

While the first of these perceptions is what we might reasonably expect to hear from satellite TV consumers, since the technology has been marketed in terms of increased 'freedom' of choice for viewers, the second is less predictable. Mr Harvey explains that:

> When I'm watching Sky – because it's from a European satellite – and when I'm looking at some of the other continental stations that are available, I very much get the sense of being a European. A lot of the channels are an hour ahead, they're on European time. If you're just channel-hopping, which is a bit of a sport for me – buzzing round eight or nine stations to see what's going on – you do get the feeling of not being restricted in the good old British way. It's quite something when you can sit down in your own front room and watch what's on in another country.

The opposition he constructs between restriction and mobility is mapped on to another distinction in which Britishness and 'Europeanness' are contrasted. His viewing pleasures could be seen to constitute a kind of armchair 'televisual tourism'. Satellite TV is helping him travel, electronically at least, to new places – 'channel-hopping' in a double sense of the term. Of course, as I argue elsewhere in this book, the image spaces produced by a communication technology cannot reshape subjectivities on their own. It is only when those audio-visual territories are articulated with existing situations and discourses that a fiction such as Europe becomes a reality for particular groups of people. So Mr Harvey, who makes hi-tech goods for the export market, already identifies with an international business community. The fact that his parents have bought a retirement home in Spain also contributes to Sam's recognition of himself as a European. Their villa is now a regular destination for family holidays abroad. Mrs Harvey, too, finds the idea of Europe has a certain limited salience. When her younger sister – a university arts student – came to visit with a boyfriend from France, they were able to show them French-language programmes on satellite television. Some of these circumstances are obviously unique to the Harvey household – whilst others, like the commercial and cultural significance of a single European market, will have far wider currency.

The theme of 'modern versus traditional' runs just as powerfully through pursuits and disputes in the Harveys' home as it did through the Gibsons'. In this family, it is the father who is a self-confessed 'gadgeteer'. From the stage at which he began playing around with lightbulbs and electrical circuits as a teenager, Sam has always been enthusiastic about technology. He can be located within what Leslie Haddon (1988) has called 'hobbyist' culture, a predominantly masculine sphere of social activity where consumers are concerned to experiment with all the latest innovations in IT. Their house currently contains three computers – one of which he assembled himself out of bits – two video recorders and two TVs, in addition to the satellite system and a CD player. An interest in electronic music has also resulted in plans to purchase a synthesiser. Liz, however, is conscious that 'people do take the mickey out of us … we're constantly tripping over monitors and things'. Her feelings towards these gadgets are more ambivalent than those of her husband. Indeed, she is clearly frustrated about money being spent on his 'toys', since this means it goes unspent on her preferred pastime of collecting antique furniture.

If this family's interpersonal dynamics and patterns of taste appear to be organised chiefly along gendered lines, then it is worth highlighting relations across the generations as well – by looking at the ties which Mr and Mrs Harvey have with their children, and at tensions that arise when Liz's parents come to stay. Although the youngsters are denied access to certain areas of domestic space, including the front room in which satellite television is watched, that does not mean they are kept away from media technologies altogether. On the contrary, the older VCR was 'given to the kids' and Sam's microcomputer from college days has now been handed down to the five-year-old, Phil. These are very good illustrations of what has been referred to as the 'cultural biography' of objects (Kopytoff 1986; Silverstone et al. 1992), where a technology's position and function within the home are shifting, and where its 'career' can be traced against the changing biographies of household members.

Goods and competences in this household are passing through a gradual process of 'inheritance'. Mr Harvey proudly reports to me on his son's progress with the micro: 'He knows how to put discs in, knows what disc drives are and can operate them ... which is great because I'd like him to get into computing'. Predictably, Liz is less sure how she feels about Phil's acquisition of his father's enthusiasm for electronic gadgetry. She readily acknowledges the educational advantages of a technological literacy – yet describes Phil, with some regret, as 'a child of the nineties'. Her own recent efforts to hand on nostalgic pleasures to the children ended in disappointment. Mrs Harvey purchased a video tape of the BBC's original *Watch with Mother* broadcasts as a gift for them, only to find that they found it slow and boring in comparison with modern American cartoon shows like *Teenage Mutant Hero Turtles*.

Meanwhile, Mrs Harvey's parents have taken exception to the satellite dish which is mounted on the house exterior. It has even been the source of arguments between mother and daughter when they come to visit. 'My mum thinks it's rather vulgar', Liz explains. 'She says to me, "You really shouldn't have that thing on the front of such a lovely Edwardian home".' There could be no more emphatic statement of the conflict involving discourses of innovation and conservation. Comparing the perceived ugliness of an Amstrad dish with the assumed beauty of period architecture, Liz's mother forms a critical judgement on the basis of certain moral and aesthetic values which privilege 'past' over 'present'.

We have seen how the juxtaposition of traditional and modern codes is at the root of several frictions in this domestic context. Mrs Harvey's desire for pieces of antique furniture is opposed to Sam's fascination with electronic gadgets. Similarly, the uncertain feelings she has about Phil learning to use a microcomputer contrast with Mr Harvey's evident pride in his son's interest and initial achievements. As for the disagreement between Liz and her parents over the dish aerial on the front wall, she chooses temporarily to side with her husband – reluctantly identifying with the modern, because she is forced on to the defensive by their unfavourable comments. In these different situations, she must skilfully negotiate the contradictions of her gendered and generational subject positions as they are related to particular senses of old and new.

Both Mr and Mrs Harvey tell me they are amused by her parents' remarks on the satellite dish – and yet there are strong indications that they, too, are anxious over its appearance. So although Sam sees it as a symbol of technological progress, a sign of them being 'ahead of the times', he worries simultaneously about the connotations this object may have for others. He admits that if they were to put the property on the housing market in the near future, he would seriously consider taking the dish aerial down 'if it proved detrimental to the sale of the house'. As Liz confesses, 'most of the people we know do actually think it's a bit vulgar'. Also, a local city councillor has been distributing leaflets to residents in the district – asking for people's opinions on the spread of dishes – and this kind of public consultation could have added to their discomfort.

This extract from my interview with the Harveys clearly demonstrates the concern they have over the positioning and visual impact of the dish, which Sam installed himself, on the housefront:

> *Liz*:  We did try to put the dish round the back, didn't we? ...
>   Still, I don't think it's as bad – as noticeable – on our house
>   as it is on some where there's just a straight row of houses in
>   a line. Then it can look awful.
>
> *Sam*:  Yes. If it was out at the end of the bay, it'd be apparent
>   from all directions – whereas, at the moment, you can actually
>   come down the road and not realise it's there.

It is interesting to compare the sentiments expressed above with the opinions which were voiced by Mr Gibson. He believed dish aerials on modern 'prefabricated' buildings to be less of an eyesore than those on traditional Edwardian structures. Mrs Harvey has a different view, but only because she thinks the stone bay fronts help to hide them better. What Liz and Sam share with Mr Gibson is a wish for the things to be made 'invisible'.

## Other Households

Listening to the accounts given by other households in the same neighbourhood, it is possible to hear a whole range of 'resonances' with those cultural processes that are at work in the Gibson and Harvey families. In the two portraits presented so far, close attention has been paid to the ways in which electronic media get stitched into the fabric of daily domestic life, particularly how satellite TV is approached by family members with varied dispositions. The part played by this technology in helping to articulate new senses of collective identity was also discussed – and I have insisted that field research carried out in specific locales might provide us with valuable material for reflecting upon larger, more global, questions of community. Lastly, my analysis has explored the multiple and contested significance of satellite dishes in a certain residential setting – including the mixed feelings of pride, disgust or embarrassment which are evoked by these artefacts. Pursuing themes developed over the preceding pages, I now go on to offer some further, selected examples from the data – in order to 'amplify' this ethnographic reading of satellite television's meanings in Neighbourhood A.

My interviews and observations confirm that there is a definite pattern of satellite TV being desired and acquired by male consumers. Only in one family, the Clarks, have I come across a situation in which the woman was responsible for the decision to buy a dish – and in this case, it was a mother giving her thirteen-year-old son a special gift at Christmas. The boy, a keen follower of the satellite sports coverage, always used to be out watching at a friend's house before the Clarks got their own domestic receiver. His mother wanted him to spend more time at home, and saw satellite television as a means to that end. Programmes on the Eurosport and Screensport channels are the main attraction for two men living elsewhere in the neighbourhood, Mr Morgan and Mr Lloyd. Against their wives' wishes, they have each bought dish aerials which enable them to see soccer or boxing matches that are not shown on the existing terrestrial stations:

> *Mr Morgan*: I was the one who wanted to have it. She didn't want me to have it at all. I was watching sport all the time and she didn't like it. It cost us two hundred pounds. That was the other thing she didn't like – the money it cost – but I won in the end, I always do.

> *Mrs Lloyd*: He got it for the sports channels.
> *Mr Lloyd*: The boxing ... they've got a lot on there which you don't get on the ordinary television. It's on nearly every night.
> *Mrs Lloyd*: I didn't want to have it. I was very much against it, but I had to get used to it.

Mrs Lloyd is a regular viewer of the evening soap operas on BBC and ITV – programmes which her husband dismisses as 'rubbish' –

and since the arrival of satellite TV, these have had to be seen on an old television set in the back room. She does admit, though, that: 'Some afternoons ... if I'm ironing and things, I'll watch a film on Sky ... I like films about romance, things that he doesn't watch ... he watches all the macho movies'.

There is also a further instance of a young gadget collector in his bedroom, echoing the experiences of Tony Gibson. Steve Price, a merchant sailor in his early twenties, still lives in an upstairs flat at the parental home for several months of the year when he is not at sea. With the money he earns, Steve has put together an expensive hi-fi system and owns two VCR machines in addition to the satellite television equipment. He mostly tunes in to the rock videos on MTV. By contrast, and in common with Mr and Mrs Gibson, his mother and father 'never watch it ... they're not interested, they get the ordinary channels on their set downstairs'.

This young man, much like Sam Harvey or Tony, talks about feeling 'limited' by the stations which are available from terrestrial broadcasting services. His work in the merchant navy took him to the United States where he witnessed multi-channel cable systems first hand. Steve's acquisition of satellite TV on returning to the UK was an attempt to reproduce that experience: 'I've watched quite a bit of TV over there, and thought the more the merrier, you know – a wider variety – which is why I bought it'. The sign of 'America' is prominent here – rather than the idea of Europe – but the principles of travel and mobility, either actual or imaginary, are present again. There has, of course, been a long history of debates concerning the export of American styles and texts to Britain (see Hebdige 1982; Tomlinson 1991) – with some social groups branding US culture as vulgar and others choosing to celebrate it. Instead of making such judgements, it is the ethnographer's task to seek out those inter-discursive moments of connection where transnational identifications are forged. More of these moments will be considered in the following section of the chapter.

Anxiety over the public display of dishes, evident in my family portraits, is expressed by other consumers in this neighbourhood. Mrs Clark, the woman who purchased a satellite receiver for her son, found that she and her husband worried about the dish's appearance when it was fitted to the front of their home:

> I wanted it to go on the back ... they're a bit unsightly and nobody else in the street has got one, except one house where they've got one round the back so you don't notice. It's not so bad, though, because we've got it above the porch – it doesn't stick out so much there.

Similarly, Steve Price confesses to having had second thoughts after installing a dish by himself at his parents' house. 'I do wonder if it looks a bit out of place', he reflects, 'because the local council have painted the old railings and made the park nice, I suppose that's why'.

It is the now familiar opposition between innovation and conservation which provokes Steve's doubts, and this conflict of cultural tastes functions in the Morgans' home as well. While the husband usually gets his way in disputes over the acquisition and use of media technologies, the wife controls decisions in the domain of interior decoration. Mrs Morgan has created an 'antique look' in the lounge with traditional ornaments and furnishings, alongside a fireplace that she had specially restored for the room. Her general opinion of satellite television is low, and there are concerns over how the dish aerial is interpreted by middle-class people living in their street. Mr Morgan, a lorry driver, refers to the views of a teacher's wife across the road: 'She thinks it lowers the tone of the area with a dish out the front ... there's a lot of doctors and teachers round here, and I don't think they're keen on them'. As for his own perception, Mr Morgan is less anxious than most interviewees in the district. 'Why worry?', he asks. 'Life's too short, isn't it?' In fact, his expression of indifference to the dish has more in common with the responses, or rather the lack of them, recorded in my working-class neighbourhood – the findings from which are reported below in the chapter's final section. There, the erection of dishes seems relatively unproblematic.

## Neighbourhood B: Detached with Drives

Neighbourhood B is a suburban area located some eight to ten kilometres from the middle of the city. Bounded by parkland and a by-pass road, and with a boating lake at its centre, the district contains predominantly detached or semi-detached housing which was built in the inter-war period. Houses are set back from the road with their own drives and gardens, and they are among the city's more expensive properties. As we might expect, the local population is chiefly made up of middle-class professional households. Of the three neighbourhoods featured in my study, this had by far the fewest satellite dishes on public display – and in order to find people to interview, I spent a considerable amount of time walking around the area in search of dish aerials before approaching households and negotiating access. However, once inside the private sphere, I found these interviewees to be the most vocal of all – keen to reflect on their own cultural experiences.

Instead of constructing discrete family portraits like those that were presented in the previous section of the chapter, I employ thematic subheadings under which my data on particular households can be considered and compared. The personal circumstances of respondents are discussed as I go along. A first major theme running through my interview material has to do with the regulation of the home's boundaries, and the role that communication and information technologies play in routine practices of 'boundary maintenance'. Secondly, there is the related theme of travel – physical and imaginative – to places, spaces and times beyond the immediate confines of the domestic realm. This leads us back again to issues of collective identity, and the concept of 'reach' is used here as a way of describing and analysing TV viewers' identifications with various territories of broadcast transmission. Finally in this section, articulations of gender and technology are revisited in an attempt to account for the peculiarly masculine formation which I am choosing to call 'gadgeteer culture'.

## Boundaries In and Around the Home

For individual household members and for the domestic group as a whole, boundary marking is of crucial importance in the ongoing production and experience of home. The boundaries may be external 'frontiers' with the public world outside or internal divisions within the private domain. They can be spatial or temporal, material or symbolic, but each of them is caught up with particular constructions of identity and difference – and they might be tied to dynamics of authority and resistance, or to feelings of 'security' and 'anxiety'. Resources which enable such social and psychological boundaries to be drawn include those made available by the electronic media (Silverstone and Morley 1990; Hirsch 1992) – by television, of course, but also by other technologies. So in the following accounts of consumption, as in the last section, I have not restricted myself to talking solely about satellite TV. Rather, I seek to develop a wider perspective on media use in household contexts – on the meanings of machines like telephones, computers, video and hi-fi equipment – seeing a new broadcasting service as deeply embedded in the structures and textures of day-to-day life.

The boundary between home and work provides us with an appropriate point of departure for this discussion of the six households that were visited in Neighbourhood B, since it has a salience for all the interviewees here. Of special interest are instances where paid work is done from home, and where the separation therefore requires some careful negotiation. For example, we could take the case of the Bennetts – a middle-aged, married couple with no dependent children who describe themselves to me as working 'on opposite sides of the fence'. Mr Bennett is a tax inspector who goes out to work during the day, whilst his wife is a self-employed accountant who operates out of her upstairs office at home. For him, the division is quite clearly drawn. However, Mrs Bennett has difficulties in keeping apart the two sides of her life, which she conducts in the same domestic place.

Technologies figure prominently in her efforts to manage the situation, none more so than the phone. Mrs Bennett needs this technology to speak to clients about the accountancy work, yet she announces angrily that:

> I hate the damn thing. Clients think that, because you're working from home, you're a twenty-four hour service – which I'm definitely not ... I want to talk to people when I want to talk to them. It's the intrusion I don't like ... I only want an interruption on my terms. I object to being rung up early on a Saturday morning, or at half past eleven at night. I suppose it's because – having had a couple of late night phone calls in the past with bad news – if the phone rings late at night or very early in the morning, then I hate it. It really knocks me for six. Well, I just unplug the phones now. There's no phone on in this house at the moment, and the answering machine's shut down as well. It goes off at around eight o'clock. So evenings, and all weekend, the phones are unplugged.

The tactics she has adopted to defend her domestic privacy against intrusions may seem extreme, although they are an understandable response to the problem of definition which Mrs Bennett faces. To borrow a popular home-as-castle metaphor, we could say that a 'drawbridge' is being pulled up on her working day or week when she goes through the ritual of unplugging the telephones.

In complete contrast, let us consider the case of Mike Rocheteau – also an accountant by training – who runs his own hi-tech business planning service from an office at the top of the large detached property which he shares with his wife and their two-year-old daughter. For Mike, the significance of the telephone is reversed. There are four lines in the office, including a fax and modem link, and a mobile phone goes with him whenever he is out of the house. Additionally, there is an answering machine that is always switched on. He confesses: 'I've got a phobia about it, about other people not being able to speak to me ... I'm available seven days a week, twenty-four hours a day'.

Rather than putting up defensive barriers, Mike prefers to use telecommunications to construct a constantly 'permeable' external boundary to the home, anxious not to lose any orders from potential customers. Yet when I turn to ask about boundaries inside their household, he speaks about a firm separation of family activity from work in the office, and admits to spending much of his time and energy on the latter in a bid to build up the business. My interview with him was actually recorded in the office space – 'the orifice', as he jokingly refers to it – where Mike explained the distinctive features of his domestic geography and routine:

> That door is very much a barrier. I keep it shut ... That's the house and this is the office ... I have very little relaxation. For me, it's all business-connected, really. I don't have much of a home life. I enjoy my business life, it's great fun ... I never don't like coming in here. This is the be-all and end-all, this room. I spend up to a hundred hours a week in here ... To me, it's not work.

Inside the office, there are three computers and a scanner – as well as colour and laser printers – with which documents are prepared for clients. Mike keeps up to date on the latest developments in computer hardware and software, subscribing to several specialist trade magazines, and he spends large sums of money acquiring equipment: 'There's forty or fifty thousand pounds' worth of kit in this room'. In terms of both technological competence and financial cost, this gives rise to certain frictions between him and his wife, Elinor. 'I've tried to get her interested in computers but she hasn't got a clue', he says, adding that 'she's a total duffer when it comes to technology'. Care is required in interpreting this claim, because his definitions of technology and skill are evidently gendered (see Cockburn 1985). In fact, elsewhere in the interview, Mike acknowledged that he rarely goes into the kitchen and has no expertise or interest in operating the machinery there. When it comes to the control of money in their marriage, there is a clear conflict between spending on the business and on the rest of the house: 'Sometimes she says we can have this but I want that, and I win 'cause I'm flipping paying ... What's in here pays for the lot, so this room's the priority'.

From my point of view as a researcher, a crucial purchasing decision to be explored was the one which had resulted in the arrival of their satellite TV system. The main television set in this household is placed in the living room downstairs. Mike watches it very little. His young daughter enjoys the Children's Channel, whilst Elinor chooses to view selected films on Sky Movies – 'she doesn't like horror, doesn't like comedies, goes for her own rubbish' – but it was still his decision to get a dish. In part, he says it was down to a general interest in new technology, although there is a more specific reason which relates to an expensive sporting hobby. He occasionally drives his own racing car in competitions at various circuits around Britain, and is a committed Formula One fan. Satellite TV was first acquired so that he could video record these events when they were broadcast on Screensport: 'I got it to see the motor racing, to see the Grand Prix live and to watch my own racing'. The high cost of such a hobby is offset by sponsorship deals and he has gained several orders for his business venture through contacts made in motor sport. Even in the pursuit of leisure, he appears to be immersed in the world of work.

Despite the very different relationships which they engineer between domestic life and the wider business community, Mrs Bennett and Mike Rocheteau do share broadly similar views of the boundaries which separate their homes from the immediate locale of the suburban neighbourhood. So when I asked Mrs Bennett to tell me what she felt about the neighbourhood, her reply was 'absolutely nothing ... I know the ducks on the lake better than I do people round here'. As a result, she and her husband had no anxieties whatsoever about whether the neighbours would object to their satellite dish. 'They don't interfere with us and we don't interfere with them', she explained. Mike's neighbours, on the other hand, did interfere when he erected his dish on the front of the house:

> I was the first one to have it in my road. We had some quite pointed comments ... we were 'bringing the tone of the area down' ... They didn't like it, people weren't happy with the satellite dish. It's an Amstrad and people thought we had a Dixons mentality or something ... I used to wind the neighbours up, saying I was going to get a bigger dish. I don't give a toss ... someone said they were extremely pissed off with the satellite dish. That was when I turned round to them and said, 'You ain't seen nothing yet'.

Listening to this story of 'taste warfare', we can hear echoes of discourses which were audible in Neighbourhood A too, yet the response here to anti-dish rhetoric is a much more 'detached' and self-confident dismissal of other people's preferences or opinions.

Precisely that sort of response is offered by Paul Thomas, an unmarried, thirty-year-old civil servant. I enquired if he was worried what the neighbours thought of his Amstrad Fidelity dish. 'It doesn't worry me at all', he insisted. 'It's up to me. You're allowed to have one without planning permission, so whatever they thought they couldn't do a thing.' His initial encounter with satellite broadcasts was at the home of a colleague who lives in a small town up the valley, where cable television had been available for some years. Indeed, the regular contact with male peers in the workplace context was a crucial factor in his acquisition and use of the technology. In the office where he works, there is a good deal of talk about both the hardware and software of satellite TV. Video cassettes of taped material are often exchanged and discussed. He particularly enjoys sports programmes, rock music shows, horror and action movies – 'Schwarzenegger, Stallone, that sort of thing' – and confesses that some colleagues watch late-night pornographic films on a German-language channel. Just as Dorothy Hobson (1989) identified a feminine culture of 'gossip' based on soap-opera viewing by women workmates, so it is possible for us to point to a masculine equivalent in this office peer group of which Paul is a member.

Meanwhile, for Andy Lovell, there has long been an intimate connection between work and leisure activities. Andy, who is in his forties, owns and runs a small chain of stores selling specialist audio equipment – and before that, he worked as a sales assistant for hi-fi shops in the West of England. As I explain in greater detail later, he has a passion for music and audio technology which dates back to his teenage years. Although his home is not a workplace in the way that it is for Mrs Bennett or Mike Rocheteau, the front lounge of his spacious detached house is currently serving as a private 'showroom' in which he displays and demonstrates top-of-the-range equipment for valued clients. At present, there is a twenty-five-thousand-pound Linn stereo system in that room: 'I believe the best way to sell it is to have it in this environment. In fact, I sold one of these systems last week to some people who came and sat and listened to it'.

He lives with his partner, Cheryl – they met each other through the business – and since the addition of a 'granny flat' extension, with his mother also. Gendered and generational relationships in this household are articulated with, and by, particular divisions of interior space and uses of communication technologies. Andy and Cheryl share the same tastes in pop and classical music, but she sometimes finds the volume at which he plays his records far too loud for comfort, so will often watch TV in the back lounge whilst he listens to the hi-fi across the hall. With the sound turned up high, he cannot hear the telephone in the kitchen and keeps a mobile constantly by his side in case of any important messages. Like Mike Rocheteau, he likes to be available throughout the day, saying of his portable phone: 'People at work joke that I'll need it surgically removed from my ear'. When Andy watches television together with Cheryl, his preferences are for news, sport and comedy. During her periods of 'solo viewing', 'she loves to watch a lot of the American stuff on Sky ... and dramas like *Casualty*'. All the TVs in the house, including the set situated in the granny flat, are wired to receive satellite channels – yet his mother remains largely indifferent to the new programmes that are on offer.

Joe Mahoney, a seventy-year-old pensioner living alone, was the only elderly person I came across who actively acquired a satellite dish – though he did so under pressure from his two daughters and their respective husbands. After retirement and the death of his wife, they persuaded him that the film channels would 'help to while away the evenings'. The daughters' own families, based nearby, already had satellite television and felt it would be a comfort to him. In the event, he reports, 'I don't think I've watched a complete film since I got it'. However, he is a frequent media user. As well as a music centre and VCR, his home has TV sets located in each of the places he occupies routinely – including the bedroom, kitchen, dining and sitting rooms. Switching on the television marks a temporal boundary at the start of his day: 'It's the first thing I do ... it's an automatic thing. It's my company, somebody in the house with you'. TV keeps him 'company', too, when he has difficulty getting to sleep late at night – the time he usually watches Sky News and CNN from his bed.

If much of his everyday life is spent alone within the domestic sphere, he does take holidays abroad and goes regularly with one of his sons-in-law to see matches played by the city's ice-hockey team. In addition, he has 'stop-over' visits from the grandchildren – looking after them while their parents have a night out – and Mr Mahoney reveals how these occasions are experienced by the youngsters as a pleasurable resistance to parental control:

There's a story there. The two boys ... one of them is eleven and the other is nine ... have been banned by their father from watching the wrestling on satellite TV – the WWF, you know – because he thinks there's too much violence ... So when they come to visit me, that's the first thing they'll do, run upstairs and switch on the wrestling.

Television also figures in a negotiation of power between parents and children in the last of my six households in Neighbourhood B, the Sharma family. Mr Sharma, a city estate agent with two sons – one still at school and the other now working for his father's business – had satellite TV installed partly as a 'bribe' to keep them within the confines of the home. He is a firm believer in the importance of a strong family unit and thinks they should be indoors during the evening. This reminds me of an account from the historical research which I reported on in Chapter 3, where a young fan of jazz music was strictly forbidden by her father to attend dance halls and allowed to listen instead to bands playing on the wireless. Sixty years later, the technology of broadcasting has changed yet the parental strategy remains the same. Mr and Mrs Sharma do not share their sons' tastes in film, 'adventure, gunfighting and so on', but domestic consumption of these fictions provides an opportunity for surveillance that cannot be maintained in the public space of the street or cinema. The Sky Movies channel brings the films to them, thereby 'privatising' their viewing practices.

### Discourses of Travel and Senses of Reach

We have just heard how communication and information technologies in the modern home can be implicated in the production of more or less permeable, more or less defended boundaries between private lives and public cultures. Perhaps the best examples of this were the different narratives of telephone usage, or else its deliberate non-use. There were also interesting stories about the satellite dish serving to express a detached social relationship with neighbours. I now want to look at the role of television, particularly satellite TV, in connecting inside with outside – in turning the household into what Anthony Giddens (1990) would call a 'phantasmagoric' place, penetrated by symbolic goods which are distributed on a national or transnational scale. My commentary on the data tries to assess the consequences of these shifting media flows for senses of cultural identity, although it is necessary for us to bear in mind the complex and potentially contradictory nature of links between the local and the global, where identifications are being formed and transformed. The idea of travel or transportation may offer a valuable way of thinking about that process – an idea discussed further in Chapter 5 – along with the related concept of reach, which I am borrowing from Roger Silverstone's writing on television in daily life (Silverstone 1994). His application of the term refers to the capacity of TV, and other types of electronic mediation, to provide a 'technological extension' of social interaction across situational boundaries – helping to reconfigure the imaginative geography of culture and community.

Let us revisit the Bennetts at this point, because we are able to see how much of their lives is concerned with travel in the literal sense of the word. They tell me that they spend a large proportion of their leisure time either planning, going on or reflecting back on holidays and short breaks away. As Mrs Bennett says:

> We've only got one great love and that's travelling ... I mean we're the sort of people who don't go out for the evening – we're not pub goers – so when we go out, it's got to be grand. A few weeks ago, we went to New York for the weekend ... there's a difference between an evening out and actually going somewhere.

In recent years, they have taken trips to other destinations in the United States and travelled in Africa, Asia and Europe too. Their living room is decorated with an assemblage of ornaments, pictures and 'exotic' souvenirs which they have gathered together from these various places. For them, the 'tourist gaze' (Urry 1990) is experienced at home as well as abroad – in the pleasure they get from the visual mementos, but also in their reading of brochures and guide books, and their viewing of television holiday programmes. During the interview I conducted at their house, they were recording a round-the-world TV travelogue presented by the comedy actor Michael Palin.

However, the ties between television and travel do not stop there. As contestants on numerous TV game shows – including *Fifteen to One*, *Crosswits* and *One False Move* – the Bennetts have won holidays in America and Spain. A motivation for participating in those shows in the first instance was the opportunity which it afforded them for travelling to different cities around Britain. Television production companies have paid for their hotel accommodation where the programmes are made. For example, Mrs Bennett informs me that: 'We went to Newcastle to do *Crosswits*, hosted by Tom O'Connor ... It's a beautiful city and we'd never have thought of going there if it hadn't been for the show'.

They insist that their home satellite TV system would never have arrived had it not also been given to them as a prize, although there are now certain channels and programmes which they watch routinely. Their satellite viewing preferences are related again to the theme of travel, across both time and space. So the Bennetts enjoy repeats of classic comedies and historical dramas on the UK Gold channel. 'There are a few things on there which we'd always thought would be nice to look back at', notes Mr Bennett, 'like *Duchess of Duke Street*, because it's very well acted and represents an interesting era'. The meanings they take from these programmes are primarily nostalgic ones, involving a remembrance of their own past or else an identification with particular periods in history. Late at night, too, they stay up to watch CNN and ABC news broadcasts in order to sustain their sense of 'trans-Atlantic reach':

> *Mr Bennett*: You get ABC from America ... we like to know what's going on over there, and the satellite keeps you up to date as it happens ... We were in New England last year. The people were genuinely friendly.
>
> *Mrs Bennett*: We'd done so much travelling in the Far East and Africa, and we wanted to see more of the States.
>
> *Mr Bennett*: Watching things on CNN and ABC keeps us in touch.

Exactly how this maps on to feelings of collective identity is a complex matter. Despite their shared interest in all things American, they feel Welsh 'when it comes to rugby matches on TV', and yet this couple are reluctant to be identified abroad as British 'because of the lager louts and the crimplene frocks'. When visiting the continent, they are pleased to be mistaken for Germans – since Mr Bennett is a competent German speaker – but their political opinions on Europe are surprisingly close to those of the 'Eurosceptics' in Britain. Clearly, the same social subjects in different cultural contexts can identify themselves with varied imagined communities.

A seemingly more straightforward linkage between ethnic iden-tity, political position and viewing preference is expressed by Mr Sharma, although his case is not without its contradictions either. Born in India during the 1940s, he migrated to the UK as a young man to train as a mining engineer, eventually becoming underground supervisor of a South Wales colliery. He had spells working abroad in North America and Africa, before returning to Britain with his family to set up a property business. Mr Sharma has been actively involved in party politics, standing as a candidate for the Labour Party in European elections some years ago, and he takes a close interest in issues relating to the local Asian community. Like Joe Mahoney, he is a regular viewer of CNN and Sky News, and his generally positive opinion of satellite broadcasting is framed by a negative definition of it as – in his words – 'not the BBC'. Here, he contrasts modes of direct address in terrestrial and satellite tele-vision news:

> With the BBC, you always feel as though the structure of society is there, the authority. Their newsreaders speak just like schoolmasters. They're telling you, like schoolmasters telling the kids. I think Sky News has more of a North American approach, it's more relaxed. They treat you like equals and don't take the audience for a bunch of small kids.

If he believes firmly in parental control within his own family, then he most certainly rejects what he perceives to be the authoritarian structure of British society, which is seen as embodied in the BBC as an institution. His sympathies towards Sky, unusual at the time of our interview for somebody on the political left, are underpinned by a broader 'anti-establishment' perspective – around which an unholy alliance was later to develop between Tony Blair's New Labour and Rupert Murdoch's multinational media empire. Of course, Mr Sharma's interpretation of the technology and its broadcast forms only starts to make sense to us when we relate it to the rest of his lived experience. He already holds certain opinions arising out of his geographical situation, both as an immigrant and an emigré, and out of his involvement with politics. Satellite television enables him to connect and voice those positions in a particular fashion.

Mr Mahoney agrees that the Sky News channel has an American 'flavour', comparing it with CNN: 'I think the CNN coverage is superb. In fact, in my mind, Sky News is a bit of a replica – the same style – the man and the woman presenting, the chat between them and so on'. He has ties with North America which reach back half a century, having worked in Canada for fifteen years at an earlier stage in his life. Although he considers himself to be British, 'in as much as I'm not a Welsh nationalist', Joe retains Canadian citizenship and his two daughters were born whilst he and his wife were living there. Holidays now are often spent on the other side of the Atlantic, 'Florida or somewhere else in the States, and back to Canada to see my brother'. His musical tastes are for jazz and big band sounds. Over the years, he has accumulated a large collection of records and tapes of the American singer Frank Sinatra – along with live stage performances on video.

Surprisingly, in my small sample of interviewees, Mr Mahoney is not the only Canadian I spoke with in Neighbourhood B. Mike Rocheteau was brought up by French-speaking parents in Quebec before moving to Britain in his late teens to study for a degree in accountancy and economics. He spent time working in Germany, returned to Canada for a short spell, and now thinks of Wales as his adopted home:

> I feel Welsh. I'm here to stay ... I guess I like to be part of a minority. In motor racing circles, everyone knows I'm French Canadian – but they also know that I'm Welsh at heart, because this place has been good to me. My wife understands the Welsh language and speaks it moderately well. It'd be nice if my daughter learnt Welsh at school. I'd love her to be able to speak French and German too.

This cosmopolitan background and interest in languages translates itself into Mike's uses of communication technologies and his attitudes to business. Satellite television was bought partly for its novelty value, yet the idea of multi-channel viewing was already familiar from the Canadian context – where cable TV systems are widespread – and his knowledge of the German language is good enough for him 'to sit quite happily and watch touring car races with a German commentary'. He has recently received orders for work from two companies in France, one of them a major car manufacturer, and he is looking to the European single market for further clients. 'I don't like to think there are frontiers to my business', Mike explains.

### Further Reflections on Gadgeteer Culture

A final theme to be explored in this section has to do with that specific articulation of masculinity and machinery which gives rise to the figure of the gadgeteer. It is a theme I started to address in my account of Neighbourhood A – with reference to Tony Gibson, Sam Harvey and Steve Price – and I return to it here, taking Andy Lovell as my main example. In my interview with Andy, I encouraged him to tell the story of his unfolding relationship with audio technologies. What follows is merely a short extract from a much longer testimony:

> It all developed from a personal interest in music … and then, ever since I was a teenager, I've been building amplifiers and speakers and messing around … The whole sixties music thing just excited me so much. I remember cycling all the way into town to buy The Beatles' *Twist and Shout* EP … and I was always interested from an early age in maths and science, and how things worked … I got an old radiogram from some people who lived round the corner, a beautiful old … walnut radio cabinet with a fifteen inch, mains-energised loudspeaker in it. Well, I changed the record deck, changed the amplifier and then the speaker. I just changed the whole thing eventually, gradually improved it and improved it during my teens. Then … I started down the separates route – buying a separate turntable, building an amplifier, building loudspeakers. I can still remember the first true separate system I had was a Garrard turntable, the original SP25, a Teleton amplifier and a pair of Wharfdale Unit 3 speakers that came in a kit … I had a Sonotone 98 pick up cartridge in the SP25.

Two aspects of his talk are worthy of immediate note. One is the fact that gadgeteer culture can involve far more than 'consuming' technology – in this case, it entails a limited form of 'household production' and an adventurous, do-it-yourself spirit of experimentation. A further observation concerns his use of language, especially the listing of brand names and models towards the end of the passage above. As Andy took me through the history of audio hardware he has owned, his speech was frequently marked by terms from the trade and technical jargon. Like many social groups, academics included, gadgeteers maintain a sense of identity by employing a specialised vocabulary.

On occasion, Andy lapses into the language of desire when talking about machinery. This is evident when he describes his past and present motor cars. A Mercedes estate and a restored Series One E-Type Jaguar are parked outside in the drive. Of the former, he says: 'I love the feeling it gives me just to get in, sit down and close the door'. 'I've had all sorts of cars', he continues, 'Lotus, Porsche, BMWs … I've indulged my fantasies'. It is a discourse which has also been adopted by Mike Rocheteau, who adds an aesthetic dimension while reflecting on his various technological objects of desire:

> I just love gadgets … I love to be able to play with them. There's definitely a connection for me between cars, Swiss pen knives, Rolex watches – I used to have a nice big lumpy gold Rolex. The engineering in my BMW is a work of art … One of my old cars was a beaten-up Volkswagen Golf, but I absolutely loved it. There was something about that product … Again, there's my Braun calculator, it's seven or eight years old now but it's the best calculator I've ever had. It hasn't got many functions on it – but when you press the buttons, there's something tactile, it has a feel to it.

Andy himself applies the label of 'obsession' to the intense feelings he has for hi-fi equipment, and freely admits that his relationship with audio technology put severe strain on a previous marriage. He recalls how his first wife took the drastic step of cutting his credit card in half to prevent him spending all their money: 'It almost became, well it was – it is – an obsession. I had to keep buying new things'.

From his perspective, television is defined as 'lo-fi' technology. Despite a life-long interest in popular music, he is reluctant to watch the MTV satellite channel because of what he describes as the poor sound quality. However, Andy does have plans to remedy this situation in the future by acquiring a Lexicon Surround System for

the TV lounge: 'It's not cheap, of course. The processor costs a
thousand pounds, then you've got to buy a good quality amplifier
... which is six or seven hundred quid, only for audiophiles really'.
He is constantly thinking forward to his next purchase, another
characteristic of the gadgeteer, or to innovations which may be
coming on to the market.

The theoretical challenge that confronts ethnographers in these
circumstances is in trying to explain, as well as simply document,
the features of this cultural formation – paying careful attention to
the gendered character of the practices and pleasures which are being
displayed. If feminist work on viewing or reading communities for
soap opera or romantic fiction (see Brunsdon 1981; Radway 1987)
pointed to the highly contingent nature of articulations between
those genres and their female consumers, then it is important for us
to consider the specificities of gadgeteer culture, approaching that
connection between technologies and the men who use them as a
particular expression of masculine identity. Two existing pieces of
work can, in my view, help to shed light on the distinctive dynamics
of this culture. Researching relations between humans and computers, Sherry Turkle (1988) has written about the emotional worlds of
male college students who were virtuoso computer 'hackers'. Although
their activities were by no means identical to the hobbyist practices
which I am dealing with, the same obsessive ties with inanimate
objects are present. Turkle suggested that the young men she
observed were seeking intimate relationships with the machine,
ones which would give them mastery of the technology – perfect
control in a realm of safe things, free from the complexities and
ambiguities of close human ties. Indeed, the young women she
interviewed demonstrated a 'computational reticence' – not because
they were incapable of using IT, but because they were reluctant to
substitute interpersonal intimacy with a 'love' for machines. In an
essay more obviously applicable to Andy's case, cultural critic David
Punter (1986) has reflected on the masculine meanings of the stereo
record player. He regarded the gadget as a 'symbol of force'. Its
control panel with flashing lights reminded him of an aeroplane's
cockpit, and he commented that the stereo has a potential volume
which far outstrips its domestic requirements, like the car capable
of travelling at speeds much higher than it will ever reach on the
road. Traditionally feminine technologies such as the washing
machine and the hairdryer are without that kind of excess power.

## Neighbourhood C: Terraced Rows

The last of the three city neighbourhoods where I interviewed satellite television consumers is an area of red-brick terraced housing situated close to the main commercial and shopping centre, only two to three kilometres out of town. For the most part, its local residents are members of working-class families which have established roots in the region, although there is a more transient student population from the nearby university occupying rented accommodation. Property prices here are lower than those found in Neighbourhood A and Neighbourhood B, and the houses and flats in this district front directly on to the street, with either a back yard or small garden to the rear. As satellite dishes are a common sight down these terraced rows, it was not hard to locate potential households for the empirical study. However, gaining access proved difficult in some cases because several of the people I approached – while they had received a letter of introduction in advance – were unsure what to make of me. Despite my protestations to the contrary, I was often presumed to be working for a broadcasting company or else trying to sell them goods they already possessed. Of course, at one level, that response is perfectly understandable – they were making sense of my appearance at their door within a framework which was familiar to them – but where there was unfamiliarity with the very idea of academic research, it meant that the visits were quite awkward at first for researcher and interviewees alike.

A number of the issues which are central to the two preceding sections of my chapter appear to have a diminished significance for the people I spoke with in Neighbourhood C. For example, with the exception of interview material on viewing practices in a shared student flat, there was relatively little said by respondents about identifications – or 'disidentifications' – with new image spaces. Neither is there much to report on disputes and anxieties over the siting of dishes. Indeed, the satellite dish seems not to be such a contentious symbol in this particular urban area. In a specific instance where neighbours had made negative comments, that reaction was assumed by the dish-erector to result from their jealousy. Concerns over the dish aerial on the outside wall of a house are more likely to be bound up with problems regarding its technical operation rather than its aesthetic value. Two other themes emerge as highly significant, though. These have to do, first, with the economics of domestic consumption – the financial constraints and budgetary dynamics surrounding satellite TV's arrival – and, secondly, with the organisation of a household's 'cultural economy', the taste hierarchies and patterns of access to technology found in everyday social settings.

## The Economics of Domestic Consumption

Since the households described below are at less of a 'distance from necessity' (Bourdieu 1984) than those I have been discussing so far, choices about what technologies to acquire – and which cultural practices to engage in – are subject to considerable financial constraint. For the O'Grady family, then, the decision to rent a home satellite system was taken only after protracted negotiations between household members. Mrs O'Grady, who is a support worker with a local housing trust, was opposed to it from the outset because of what she saw as the unnecessary cost. It was her husband, a scrap-metal merchant, and their three children who were arguing for a dish. Mr O'Grady wanted the sports coverage – and his youngest son, Darren, was especially interested in watching the wrestling so he could talk about it the next day at school with his best mate. The decision-making process they went through appears 'democratic', yet when the dish eventually arrived the outcome was not so egalitarian:

> *Mr O'Grady*: My wife said no. She was all against it but we convinced her, said we'd all save up and put a bit in, and we'd pay for it monthly ... We try to do everything in the house by talking about it ... The kids were gonna pay fifty pence out of their pocket money, I would pay so much a week ... so we worked it out that if we all paid a tiny bit, then we could have it, like. It ended up that my wife paid it all. After a month or two, everybody stopped paying it – including myself – and my wife ended up with the bill ...
> *SM*: (To wife) Do you want to tell me your side of the story?
> *Mrs O'Grady*: I just think it's a waste of money, but I was outvoted. They all ganged up on me.

While the woman has a certain degree of independence in money matters as a consequence of her paid employment outside the home, she is ultimately left with the responsibility of settling their monthly rental account when others fail to pay up as agreed. This confirms what critical research on the distribution of material resources in marriage and families (Delphy 1984; Pahl 1990) has already shown – that the household cannot be understood simply as a unified 'unit' of consumption. Doing so serves to mask social inequalities and power relations in the domestic economy.

There are further financial tensions arising from Darren's use of the telephone. His parents caught him ringing an 089 number – a particular category of phone numbers associated with, for example, competitions and chat lines – and were not pleased with the size of the bill which followed: 'We found him phoning in for a competition ... He seems to think it's not gonna cost no money, then all of a sudden it's three or four pounds'. The father also remarks on his son's habit of telephoning a friend who lives just round the corner. 'Instead of walking round to see if he's coming out, he gives him a ring.' At the same time, Mrs O'Grady acknowledges the value of the phone in their extended family's life. She tells me how her own father will call to request that a programme on Sky is video taped for him, and she explains how the technology has enabled them to monitor the health of her sick mother-in-law who lives in a small town along the coast.

More distant 'kinkeeping calls' (see Moyal 1989) are made by Maria Williams, a nurse at the city's infirmary. She moved to Wales from Malta before getting married to Brian – a hospital plumber – with whom she has three children aged fourteen, ten and three. Maria keeps in touch with her family in Malta, and also in Australia, via the telephone. When I asked her if this proved costly, the rather defensive reply was 'they usually ring me'. The reason for her defensiveness became clearer as Mr Williams announced: 'If I had my way, I'd probably get rid of it because of the expense of the thing'. Indeed, a good deal of his talk about technologies is linked to economic concerns. Justifying their acquisition of satellite television, he compares the combined monthly cost of equipment rental and channel subscriptions with an evening's entertainment at the cinema:

> *Brian*: If a whole family were going to the cinema, it'd cost you quite a lot of money ... with five in the house, it may be more than ten pounds, so the movie channels are good. I think the subscription's worth it when you weigh it up ... It's sixteen ninety-nine now with the three channels we pay for ...
> *Maria*: We don't go out much really, do we?
> *Brian*: When you have a family with kids, it's difficult to go out anyway – and again, it's the expense.

Here, satellite broadcasting is seen as a relatively cheap private alternative to public leisure, despite the fact that its channels cost far more than those provided by terrestrial services for the price of a TV licence.

Next, the Cooks are an unemployed couple in their twenties who obtained a dish on a short-term, free-trial basis. Mr Cook has been out of a job for some time, having worked in the building trade. His wife – 'she's on free trial an' all', he jokes – cannot find work either. One of the husband's relatives, who had a home satellite system himself, was responsible for ringing a rental company on their behalf and arranging for the dish to be installed – but between my initial call at the house and the later visit when I interviewed them, the dish had been removed from its position just above their front door. As Mrs Cook revealed:

> It was just a two-week trial. I wrote back within a week to say we didn't want it ... We kept it for about five months before they came and took it ... They're so busy putting them up ... they haven't got anybody to take 'em down.

Although her story suggests they had several months' viewing at the expense of the rental company, a bill for which they would have struggled to pay, the Cooks went on to explain that there were technical difficulties which prevented them from receiving an adequate broadcast transmission for much of the five-month period: 'The picture was terrible. The dish was hanging off the wall. It was all right for a bit when they first put it in, but then the picture went all snowy'.

It is interesting to note that, for quite different reasons, two further homes in Neighbourhood C were temporarily without satellite transmissions at the times of my interview visits – although in both cases the external dish aerial was still intact. Gary Phillips, a thirty-eight-year-old clerical worker who lives alone, had his house broken into whilst he was out one night. The thieves took his colour television, video recorder and remote controls, 'it was a straight in and out job ... because that was all that got taken'. He has borrowed a friend's spare TV set to 'make do' until he can afford to replace the stolen goods, yet without a remote control device his satellite receiver is stuck on a film channel for which he has ceased to pay the subscription fee. Despite having no dependants to support, there are clearly strong financial pressures which determine his purchase or non-purchase of various communication technologies. For instance, his dish is a reconditioned BSB squarial bought off a market trader for thirty pounds. Gary chooses to buy music on cassette tapes rather than CDs: 'I think the price of them is a bit inhibiting. Left to my own devices, I won't bother with a CD player'. He does not possess a telephone, making any essential calls free of charge from work. In the kitchen, too, there is no washing machine – his clothes are cleaned by hand or taken to a launderette down the road.

Mr Kennedy, a driver for the local bus company, bought his Amstrad satellite dish second-hand from a colleague – 'my mate at work was flogging one, so I bought it off him ... it was only cheap'. When he purchased it, he also lived alone – being separated from his previous partner and their child, a six-year-old boy. His son regularly watched satellite television at the mother's house, so Mr Kennedy wanted the boy to be able to do the same while staying over at his place. In the meantime, a new partner has moved into the house with her four children from an earlier relationship. As I outline later, this has led to some interpersonal tensions and nego- tiations of power around programme choice and access to the main TV screen in the lounge. However, during my visit to their home, they were limited to viewing terrestrial channels because the internal unit for receiving satellite broadcasts was broken. 'I used to have it on the shelf and it got knocked off a few times', says Mr Kennedy. 'I'll have to wait until after Christmas now to get it mended.' The cost of the forthcoming festive season meant that he would have to postpone paying for repair work.

If membership of the household above has shifted recently, then the boundaries of home in my final case have been much more fluid from the start. Jonathan Taylor is one of nine male university students who can loosely be described as 'living' in a large flat above a shop. Three of them pay rent on rooms elsewhere in this neighbourhood, but for the routine purposes of day-to-day life they are effectively members of the same domestic group. All have middle-class backgrounds and a number of them had an English public-school education. They regularly drink in the pub across the road and have 'clubbed together' to hire satellite television:

> The agreement was that we could all be round to watch the Sky TV at any time of the day or night that we wanted, an open-door policy ... So between nine people, it was only two pounds a month each, eighteen pounds a month altogether ... Originally, the main idea behind getting satellite TV was that there'd be decent things to watch after one or two in the morning ... After going out, you know, people come in and they don't want to go to bed straight away. So you're able to turn on and watch a film for an hour, fall asleep on the sofa before you go to bed ... Also, the extra sports coverage in a household of men, that was an important thing – the fact that we were going to get all this sport – cricket World Cup, football from around Europe.

Jonathan added that their collective approach to spending and consumption extends to other practices as well as TV viewing. For example, shopping for food and the cooking of meals are organised on a communal basis. Once a week, everybody 'chucks a tenner in' for a trip to the supermarket, and meals are often shared by the whole extended group. Similarly, there is 'a lot of borrowing of clothes and tapes', with personal ownership of property not being tightly defined. They debated collectively whether or not to install a phone line: 'In the end, we realised the expense would be just horrendous, so we decided against it'.

## Taste Hierarchies and Access to Technology

In dealing with the economics of domestic consumption in these household settings, we have been focusing on questions that are principally concerned with money and its uses. Now it is necessary for us to acknowledge the existence of a parallel economy in which there circulates what Pierre Bourdieu (1984) has called cultural capital. According to Bourdieu, power is exercised in this cultural economy through the institutional legitimation of certain tastes and practices, and the denigration of other forms that are judged to be of lesser worth. The emphasis in his own writing has been on distinctions between the preferences of social classes and class fractions in their consumption of goods and services, but he had fewer things to say there about gendered or generational differences. However, those developments in reception studies which I reviewed in Chapter 2 have highlighted gender as a key indicator of taste – alongside class – when exploring the daily activities of television consumers. Of particular interest to me in this context is the work of Morley (1986), who drew our attention to related issues of control over programme choice and differential access to media technologies in the home. These issues reappear in the following report of accounts given by my interviewees in Neighbourhood C.

I begin again with the O'Gradys because they display a clear pattern of tastes and preferences which gets articulated to, and through, a specific ordering of access to the TV screen in their living room. As I have already stated, the husband is keen on televised sport. Both he and his two sons also enjoy films that the wife would not choose to watch. What is notable in the following extract from their talk about television is Mr O'Grady's implicit 'ranking' of various programmes and genres:

> *Mrs O'Grady*: I like *Casualty* and *London's Burning*, things like that ... hospital programmes, dramas. I like films that are based on a true story. Life stories, family sagas.

*Mr O'Grady*: The weepy ones, she likes. I would say me and the boys like a horror film or a science fiction thing, something like that. There was a programme on there called *Predator*, that was excellent. It's all action. I watch satellite mainly, only things I watch on ordinary TV are the news or *Minder*.

When they were quizzed about what happens if a clash occurs in the schedules, Mrs O'Grady told me: 'There's never any real argument. I mean my husband decides what we're gonna watch and we all have to watch it'.

On occasions when Mr O'Grady is not at home – he enjoys a game of darts or cards at the pub – and his wife is out working in the evenings, the three children have a hierarchy of their own in the parents' absence. This is chiefly organised in terms of age, although gender is a salient factor too – with Peter, the seventeen-year-old, 'taking charge' in place of his father. Next in line comes his brother, Darren, and then finally their younger sister. I asked who usually had possession of the remote control in these circumstances:

*Darren*: When my dad's not here, it's Peter – and when me and my sister are watching on our own, it'll be me ... My dad says to him, 'the kids are allowed to watch their programmes', but Peter keeps turning it over – watching what he wants to watch.
*SM*: How do you sort that out between you? How do you resolve things?
*Darren*: He hides the remote under the trolley or he sits on it, or he puts it on the arm of the chair and challenges me to get it.

Such domestic struggles for dominance with his big brother probably have less to do with differences in taste than with sibling rivalry. He does not share Peter's liking for heavy rock videos on MTV, yet the central issue here is their negotiation of power.

Precisely the same type of power struggle goes on around TV viewing in Mr Kennedy's household, with the stepfather signifying his dominance in the private sphere through possession of the remote – 'I pays the licence ... I watches what I wanna watch', he insists. Of his new partner's television consumption, he says only that she is 'too busy with housework to watch much telly'. Meanwhile, the children find themselves in competition with both him and each other for access to the main TV. To some extent, they manage to get around the problem by using a second set which is situated in an upstairs bedroom, and by recording material on video so as to 'time-shift' broadcasts from their original slots in the schedule. Even then, the daughter may still experience this arrangement as frustrating on occasion: 'Like if I wanna watch ... *Casualty* and he wants to see his stupid wildlife programmes, we all have to go upstairs, and he's on his own ... with the big telly'. One of the boys adds that 'the other day, I watched a film upstairs while my brother was taping down here'. The division of cultural pleasures is mapped on to a spatial 'regionalisation' of the home (see Giddens 1981), in which particular rooms are inhabited and utilised by changing combinations of people depending upon their positions within the family structure.

Pursuing this theme of control over programme choice, I return to my interview with Brian Williams and his wife, Maria – because there is a telling moment at which he misunderstands a poorly worded question of mine:

> *Maria*: If there's sport on, I end up having to watch it – the soccer or the boxing, or whatever.
> *SM*: (To husband) Is that fair?
> *Brian*: It's not fair but it's what happens.
> *SM*: No, I meant is that a fair account of how things work out?
> *Brian*: Probably so, but it's swings and roundabouts, isn't it?
> *Maria*: Normally swings.
> *Brian*: It depends what's on. I mean, if it was a special occasion sportswise, then the sport would go on.

Although he recognises the iniquity of the arrangement, his 'right' to watch a football or boxing match takes automatic precedence over any competing demands on the family TV screen. He considers live sport to be 'sacrosanct', and is supported in that judgement by his ten-year-old son who plays junior soccer at the weekends for a team which Brian coaches. As for Maria, she has to make do with watching her favourite shows during the day, when her little daughter has finished nursery but her husband and older children have not yet come home from school or work: 'I like Sky One – the afternoon programmes – you know, quiz shows, soaps and that ... I usually do my ironing ... watching the telly'. Before she goes on late shift at the hospital, Maria starts the VCR running to tape a serial or series that she will try to watch the next day, '*Prisoner Cell Block H* ... and there's *St Elsewhere* on a Monday night on Sky'. Rather than pre-setting the timer in advance, she operates their video machine by pushing the record button and leaving the tape to run. In an investigation of the VCR's domestic meanings, Ann Gray (1992) pointed to numerous such examples of women who were under-confident in handling the technology.

The findings I present have much in common with earlier ethnographic audience research in media and cultural studies. For instance, we can see a strong demarcation of gendered genre preferences. What Hobson (1980) once termed the 'two worlds' of television remain in their separate orbits around the set – with men preferring to watch action movies, sports and information-based programmes, while the women speak mainly about enjoying soap operas and other 'human interest' dramas. Of course, it is not simply a matter of different pleasures and dispositions – it has to do with the social 'valuations' which are put on various genres by household members, and with competing demands for the use of technology. Multi-channel satellite TV has inevitably increased the level of this competition. My interview material suggests that the politics of the living room are still ordered largely to men's advantage, and that power in these working-class homes gets unevenly distributed across age divisions as well.

Dynamics of reception in the student flat, occupied by Jonathan Taylor and his middle-class college friends, are evidently not the same – partly because they all share similar gendered and generational positionings, but also as a result of them jointly constructing more distanced or cynical readings of popular entertainment. So although their interest in sport is in keeping with the tastes of several male consumers in Neighbourhood C, their interpretations of the coverage on satellite television are shaped by a deep suspicion of American culture:

> We watch it sometimes in a condescending, mickey-taking way. The prime example of that is the *WWF Wrestling* … it's just completely beyond belief … just theatre … Coverage of the soccer, too, the feeling that it didn't fit in with the ethos of the game. They're trying to turn it into American football, family entertainment. The way they've done it is unashamedly American in style, and this was viewed with great disgust and disbelief.

The feeling of disgust extended to many Hollywood movies on the film channels: 'One of the things that's still said by us now is "bloody American film" and "where's the moral going to be in this one?" … They have to have some allusion to family morals, to family values'. Whereas some of the satellite TV viewers interviewed in other neighbourhoods responded positively to the sign of America – Steve Price, the Bennetts, Mr Sharma or Joe Mahoney – these students are suspicious of its influence. Like Sam Harvey and Tony Gibson, they identify with a broadly defined sense of Europeanness. 'When you're plugged into satellite, you're plugged into a European nation where Britain doesn't take centre stage', argues Jonathan. 'I mean, the MTV weather is European weather ... and the European sport's good ... it gives you a wider view of what's going on.' Whilst it would be easy for us to dismiss this interpretation of satellite broadcasting as highly selective, since much of the output is targeted at a UK audience, we must nevertheless take serious note of the sentiment which he expresses here. His own taste hierarchy and imagining of community is built around an opposition between Europe and the US which television helps him to articulate.

# V    TV, Geography and Mobile Privatisation

Whereas the two preceding chapters have reported on the detail of my empirical research into broadcasting and everyday life, this one and the next are concerned with more general theoretical matters. They each pursue, in similar ways but from different directions, issues raised by that research which have to do with the organisation of space and time in modern society. Chapter 6 focuses on Anthony Giddens's account of late modernity and applies some of his key ideas in a discussion of mediated experience. I want to begin here, though, by explaining and elaborating upon the concept of mobile privatisation found in the work of Raymond Williams (1974; 1989). My present chapter proposes that Williams's term might be used as a starting point for the development of a human geography of television and its audiences. It draws on a range of other writings too, not all of which are specifically about TV, and calls for the spatial and temporal dimensions of communication to be put firmly on the media and cultural studies agenda.

## Staying Home/Going Places

Williams (1974) saw the medium of television as both a sought-after consequence of and an effective facilitator for that distinctive lifestyle which he named mobile privatisation. When he coined this particular phrase, before declaring years later that it was among the ugliest known to him (Williams 1989), he was trying to convey precisely how TV is caught up in the 'push' and 'pull' of contemporary social existence – how broadcasting has helped to articulate 'paradoxical yet deeply connected tendencies of modern urban industrial living' (Williams 1974: 26). In part, his concept refers to an historical shift in which much of our cultural activity has retreated into household settings – what, in another context, Jacques Donzelot (1980) called the withdrawal to interior space. At the same time, it signals there are now far greater opportunities for travel and communication across distances, and vastly expanded senses of community. To quote Williams (1989: 171), the condition of mobile privatisation 'is private ... centred on the home itself, the dwelling place', yet it 'confers ... an unexampled mobility ... it is not living in a cut-off way'. He also understood certain technologies of transportation to be involved in this broad transformation. The motor car is designed to take the individual or family group to destinations beyond the confines of home and neighbourhood, combining privacy with mobility. Advances in air travel and the growth of the package holiday industry have meant that, financial resources permitting, 'you can fly ... to places that previous generations could never imagine visiting' (Williams 1989: 171). I am interested over the coming pages in how television figures in the day-to-day lives of families or households – while connecting these domestic units with various public worlds of information and entertainment at a regional, national and transnational level. As David Morley (1992) has put it, the global meets the local in the sitting room. TV consumption simultaneously combines 'staying home' and, via electronically transmitted sounds and images, 'going places'.

Assessing the significance of Williams's term, we can say first that it encourages us to position television within wider social and historical processes. In his analysis of the medium, he was careful to avoid the pitfalls of a perspective which is known as technological determinism (see MacKenzie and Wajcman 1985) – most frequently expressed in the common-sense notion that TV, or some other technology like the steam engine or the atom bomb, has 'altered our world' (Williams 1974). Rather than seeing television as an isolated invention which then had a direct influence on society, he preferred to locate it within a complex of technological innovations – in radio, photography, telegraphy and so on – which were institutionally sought after, but whose purposes were not wholly predictable in advance. Their take-up depended partly on how those developments were applied in practice by the media industry, and also on the appropriation of technologies by audiences and users in the routine contexts of daily life (Mackay and Gillespie 1992). However, in each case the technology came to satisfy an emerging cultural requirement of modernity. It enhanced a style of living that is both private and mobile.

Secondly and relatedly, I would argue there is a valuable geographical perspective on TV implied by the concept of mobile privatisation. By approaching television cultures via these themes of privacy and mobility, of home and travel, Williams was opening up important questions concerning media and time-space relations.

The rest of my chapter considers ways in which this perspective might be expanded and made more explicit. For instance, although he was certainly interested in some of the spatial and temporal divisions which urban industrial society brought into being – its creation of a domestic sphere that was separated from the places and times of paid work – Williams had nothing to say about the internal divisions of the home and power relations between women and men, or parents and children, within the private domain. In my own qualitative studies of early radio and satellite TV consumption, I touched at several points on the micro-geography of households – the distribution of activities across different areas of the home at various stages in the daily or weekly routine – and as discussed later, in the concluding section of this chapter, further investigation of people's 'time-space paths' is now needed if we are to appreciate exactly how broadcasting is woven into the fabric of quotidian life. Ethnographic research carried out by Morley (1986) and Ann Gray (1992) has looked as well at the gendered dynamics of control over viewing choices and the meanings of technology in families. That kind of critical audience inquiry enables us to fill a crucial gap in Williams's theory of television as a domestic medium.

His ground-breaking notes on the flow of TV programming did constitute an initial attempt to understand how broadcast output is tailored to fit the day-to-day circumstances of household members. These notes have been extremely helpful for the field of media and cultural studies, provoking subsequent reflection – for example, from John Ellis (1982) and Klaus Bruhn Jensen (1995) – on the ways in which television is oriented to geographically dispersed audiences. Paddy Scannell's observations on the communicative ethos of broadcasting (Scannell 1989) can also be seen to have extended Williams's original line of argument by highlighting the distinctive forms of talk employed in TV and radio. Those informal styles of speech that were previously confined to face-to-face interpersonal communication in ordinary daily settings have now become a prominent feature of mediated discourse, as private life has been gradually 'resocialised' by broadcasting. We might consider gossip, so central to soap-opera narratives, as an ordinary discursive style which TV airs publicly and relays back into our homes for privatised consumption. Similarly, contemporary television chat shows – with their increasingly improvised and self-reflexive banter (see Tolson 1991) – provide us with an illustration of this trend towards greater conversationalisation in the media. Without getting too excited about the progressive political implications of such change, I agree with Norman Fairclough (1992) that there has been a limited 'democratisation' of institutional talk in recent times.

If television is a domestic medium, then Williams (1974) was keen to stress the 'outward looking' nature of the modern home and the role played by broadcasting in mediating relationships between households and the symbolic communities within which they are positioned. TV makes available its own particular image spaces, inviting identification with cultural constituencies that transcend the narrow boundaries of localised interaction. Traditionally, its electronic territories have corresponded to the space of the nation-state. In Britain, where the very first broadcast transmissions were regional, the BBC soon defined its public-service duties as involving the promotion and maintenance of a strong national culture. The organisation has granted audiences access to a shared calendar of festivities and civic rituals (Cardiff and Scannell 1987), and has celebrated the more mundane, everyday aspects of national life through a genre like the popular news magazine (see Brunsdon and Morley 1978). Of course, there are many social contradictions and regional tensions to be negotiated in this fictioning of nation-as-community, and not all viewers will necessarily identify with the images and sounds on offer. To conceptualise the processes of iden-tification – or disidentification – that are at work, a theory of 'inter-discourse' (Pecheux 1982) or articulation (Hall 1986a) is required. We should approach national, and transnational, identities as the outcome of a continuing 'dialogue' between publicly circulated representations and the cultural dispositions of consumers in the private sphere. Expressions of community are a result of these elements being actively hitched together – a connection which is contingent and therefore can, in time, be uncoupled.

The data I presented in Chapter 4 includes specific cases in which the old articulations of nation and family are now uncoupling, as a new media technology makes it possible for quite different inter-discursive connections to be forged. For a variety of reasons, those satellite television viewers chose to identify instead with fictions of Europe or America – enjoying a heightened, if partly illusory, feeling of freedom and mobility. Admittedly, when interpreting the words of my interviewees, there is a danger of overestimating the technology's transnationalising potential and the pace of social transformation. Williams would no doubt want to warn us against letting this argument slip into a sort of futuristic technological determinism – and in debates about TV and 'Europeanisation', commentators such as Richard Collins (1990b) and Philip Schlesinger (1991) have urged caution, alerting us to the problems of any naive 'television without frontiers' thesis. Still, it is worth exploring why the idea of Europe – or the sign of America – already has relevance as an imaginary destination for certain groups of consumers, being careful to ground any grand statements about media and globalisation in empirical studies of local reception practices. What appears undeniable is that over a long period of time and in uneven patterns, the spaces of national cultures are progressively eroding. The precise consequences of this erosion are unclear, though. Transnational flows of information and entertainment are seen by some to lead inevitably to the 'homogenisation' of global culture, yet others perceive an increased 'heterogeneity' of places and hybrid local identities (see Chapter 7).

## Towards a Human Geography of Television Cultures

So far, it has been my intention to identify an implicitly geo-graphical perspective in Williams's work on TV and to begin to supplement his insights with reference to selected writings on the medium. Next, I try to develop this approach by drawing on literature which comes from further afield – from the discipline of geography itself, as well as from North American communication theory and anthropology – moving towards a revised programme for research on television and its audiences. In talking of revision, I am suggesting that there might be limitations to current perspec-tives in TV analysis – and the so-called 'British cultural studies' paradigm (see Turner 1990), out of which a number of my own research interests have grown, is a case in point. While that line of inquiry has focused usefully on the connections between texts, readers and contexts of reading, we need to 'graft' its social semiotic concern with meaning construction on to a broader model of time-space relations.

Somebody who has already attempted a similar kind of grafting or crossover is the geographer Peter Jackson (1989), whose book on 'maps of meaning' sought to bridge the gap between his own discipline and the concerns of cultural studies. Referring to the early work of Stuart Hall and others at the Centre for Contemporary Cultural Studies in Birmingham, and to the writings of Williams – but not to the notes on television and mobile privatisation – Jackson advocated a critical, interpretative geography of culture. The book's strength lies in its detailed reading of city landscapes, demon-strating how the design and occupation of urban places relates to a politics of class, sexuality and ethnicity. Unfortunately, its main weakness is a failure to deal adequately with the spatio-temporal implications of electronic media – the potential which they have to help reconstitute our imaginative mappings of the social world. He mentioned in passing that experiences of space and time are 'now thoroughly mediated by ... what we see on television' (Jackson 1989: 22), whilst acknowledging that geographers have had a tendency to neglect the role of media technologies in modern life.

After the publication of Jackson's book, there were several academics based in the discipline of geography who started to pay more attention to the media. For instance, Andrew Leyshon (1995) discussed the spatial and temporal dimensions of a dramatic speed-up of communications over the past one hundred and fifty years – the part which transportation and information technologies have played in 'shrinking' the globe, at least for those privileged individuals and social groups who have sufficient resources to access such services. Some human geographers also looked at what they called the 'collapsing' of space and time (see Brunn and Leinbach 1991), pointing – amongst other things – to extensive airline connections, multi-channel TV, the diffusion of satellite dishes and the rapid delivery of telephone messages. In turn, these notions of shrinkage and collapse echo what is perhaps the best-known concept to have emerged from contemporary geographical thought, the idea of 'time-space compression' (Harvey 1989). David Harvey coined this phrase in an effort to express the sense that our spatial and temporal worlds are being continually compressed or squashed smaller. Although his central focus was not on the electronic media, Harvey (1989: 293) observed how 'satellite communication makes it possible to experience a rush of images from different spaces almost simultaneously ... on a television screen'. Unlike Giddens, whose ideas on space and time are reviewed in the following chapter, he saw these technical and cultural developments giving rise to a distinctively 'postmodern condition' which incorporates aesthetics of fragmentation and simulation.

When Jackson indicated that the media had been largely neglected by those in his discipline, he referred at the same time to a notable exception – a pioneering collection of essays, edited by Jacquelin Burgess and John Gold (1985), on geography and popular culture. One of the contributions to this volume (Brooker-Gross 1985) examined changing conceptions of place in the history of news reporting. The author was concerned to chart the initial impact of electronic communication on the form and reach of news coverage, and her piece provides a convenient link with the next part of my discussion since she derived analytical inspiration from the historical work of Harold Innis, an important figure in North American communication theory (see Ferguson 1990). As Susan

Brooker-Gross explained, Innis (1951) had made a general distinction between 'time-biased' and 'space-biased' communication. In societies characterised by the former, a durable and deeply rooted sense of place was created, the archetype here being an oral culture. By contrast, the latter is thought to offer a comparatively 'placeless' existence. Modern media technologies, ranging from the telegraph to satellite television, help to constitute 'communities ... not in place but in space, mobile, connected over vast distances by appropriate symbols' (Carey 1989: 160).

The sort of approach which was taken by Innis – and later popularised by fellow Canadian Marshall McLuhan (1964) – could be criticised for its failure to address the actual content of media messages and for its leanings towards technological determinism, yet it must not be dismissed too easily on these grounds because it does serve to emphasise issues of space and time in the study of communication. Joshua Meyrowitz (1994) has proposed that these scholars should be labelled retrospectively as 'medium theorists'. He chose this name for them as their writings are concerned primarily with the communicative properties of any particular medium or technology, and with its function in the organisation of a society. Indeed, Meyrowitz described himself as a second-generation medium theorist. Citing Innis and McLuhan as two of his major influences, he had published a book on media and social behaviour (Meyrowitz 1985) which asked how the electronic transmission of information via TV and other technologies is altering patterns of interaction and the geography of everyday life. Whilst I find myself doubting some of the specific conclusions which he reached – for example, that television has been a progressive force in reshaping old-established divisions of gender and generation – I have no trouble accepting his general proposition that symbolic interactions today are not always dependent upon the co-presence of participants, nor are they necessarily limited to a single physical setting. As a result, the home 'is now a less bounded ... environment because of family members' access and accessibility to other places ... through radio, television and telephone' (Meyrowitz 1985: vii). Whether this communication at a distance translates directly into an experience of placelessness, as Meyrowitz suggested, is highly debatable. It certainly changes the relationship between settings and opens up possibilities for new formations of culture and community.

For cultural anthropologists, whose research traditionally involved the in-depth ethnographic study of a situated locale, the transformed geography of place in modern society led to a theorisation and empirical investigation of what has been termed 'the shifting anthropological object' (Olwig and Hastrup 1997). Among those who have begun to problematise place in this way are James Clifford (1992) and George Marcus (1992). Clifford, then, has encouraged anthropologists to rethink their traditional objects of inquiry as a consequence of new relations between the local and the global. His contention was that the ethnographer can no longer confidently delimit a bounded site or 'field' for research, because late twentieth-century culture is better grasped by metaphors of mobility and displacement than by the notion of a fixed location. He therefore advocated the study of 'travelling cultures' – of different movements, both physical and imaginative, which are made in and out of places – and he understood broadcasting as a means of travel through geographical space. Marcus (1992: 315) advanced a similar position, remarking that the 'production of identity ... does not depend alone, or even always primarily, on ... observable, concentrated activities within a particular locale'.

Although their critiques are targeted at the classic anthropological method, in which a concrete local context such as the 'native village' was assumed to constitute the field, the words of Clifford and Marcus are just as pertinent to academics in media and cultural studies who are conducting ethnographies of domestic television consumption. Those of us who investigate the household uses of communication technologies, analysing the interpersonal dynamics of media reception, must also recognise the permeability of the home's boundaries (see Allan 1989a) – the constant 'to-and-fro' of bodies, sounds and images across the threshold between private and public domains. Having said that, we do have to start somewhere. As I argue at the end of Chapter 8, my own preference is still for research which is ultimately grounded in the daily practices of social subjects in specific locations – but only on condition that these practices are treated as a foundation from which to explore the many distant or virtual sites that people visit via transport and electronic media.

### Directions for Research

Pulling together the various threads of my discussion, I now want to conclude by outlining three main directions for research in this proposed human geography of TV cultures. First, we need to chart some of the time-space paths and biographies of television viewers – attending to movements in and through physical locations, both inside and outside the household, throughout the day and week across months or even years. Such a 'time-geography' of social activity (see Gregory and Urry 1985) would enable us to examine the complex yet strongly patterned networks of interaction which people are constructing for themselves. Acknowledging the problems of administering time-use research, its value for that sort of purpose has already been recognised by certain academics in media and cultural studies (Silverstone et al. 1991). Questions about who routinely watches what with whom, employing which modes of consumption and making which meanings or pleasures, should continue to interest ethnographers of domestic TV reception – although a greater emphasis on the spatial and temporal contexts of that consumer behaviour and response is required. In addition, future work on television audiences could draw on the techniques of 'longitudinal analysis' developed in the 1990s by a team of researchers associated with the British Film Institute (Petrie and Willis 1995; Gauntlett and Hill 1999). Their innovative methodology, which incorporated elements of a life-history approach, has delivered rich data on TV's changing role in the lives of individuals and households. Presenting findings from a five-year 'audience tracking' study that solicited written accounts over this period from over four hundred and fifty viewers in the UK, they reported on the impact of life-cycle transitions – like getting married, having children, changing jobs and then retiring – on engagements with the medium. Rather than taking synchronic snapshots of everyday life, they sought to focus on diachronic cultural processes.

The second direction which I have in mind would involve us in further investigation of the professional cultures and communicative techniques of television. We need to understand better the efforts of those working within the TV industry to overcome physical and social distances that separate them from their audiences. So whilst a growing number of qualitative research projects – mine included – have been preoccupied with day-to-day settings and acts of consumption, far fewer have applied the same observational and interview methods to contexts of production as Schlesinger (1987) was able to do in his ethnographic study of BBC newsrooms. This is a pity because, despite the serious difficulties which social and cultural theorists have identified with notions of authorship and intention, the analysis of programme making must remain an important part of our attempt to come to terms with the time-space relations of broadcasting – even if the gap between producers and consumers can occasionally seem like a 'missing link', to borrow Schlesinger's words. Similarly, research on reception ought to be complemented by a continuing attention to the detail of television programme output, and especially to the linguistic features of broadcast talk. In collections edited by Scannell (1991a) and more recently by Allan Bell and Peter Garrett (1998), several contributors have shown practical ways forward here by drawing on perspectives from language studies or the sociology of interaction. Crucially, their concern has often been with the audience-oriented character of media discourse.

Thirdly, as will be clear from my arguments above – both in the present chapter and in the previous one – tracing TV's part in the creation of collective identities would be an essential element of this human geography of television and its audiences. Having referred earlier to James Carey's term, 'communities in space' (Carey 1989), I am proposing that these imagined senses of community be seen as deeply felt yet provisional ties stretched between private and public life. Existing analyses of national identity in our field have tended to concentrate on the publicly available stories and symbols of nationhood (see Formations Collective 1984; Bhabha 1990) without also going on to observe the reception and articulation of those fictions in the relative privacy of everyday social settings. A notable exception, though, is research which was carried out by Michael Billig (1992). He recorded and analysed conversational interviews with members of sixty-three households in the English Midlands, using images and perceptions of British royalty as a platform for group discussions on the themes of family and nationality. Anybody who doubts the relevance of a qualitative interview technique for investigating communities in space should consult Billig's material. I employed that method myself in studying how collective identities can be formed in particular relationships with TV technology. Where there was multiple ownership of television sets, this sometimes allowed viewers in the home to go on journeys to different destinations and to position themselves within different collectivities. To paraphrase McKenzie Wark (1994), experience in global culture is the product not only of 'roots' but of 'aerials' too.

# VI  Experiences of Media and Modernity

Anthony Giddens (1990; 1991) has done perhaps more than any other contemporary social theorist to foreground issues of space and time in the study of modern society. He had developed an interest in these issues whilst elaborating his influential theory of structuration (see Urry 1991), which was concerned to reconcile different traditions of sociological thought on the problems of 'agency' and 'structure'. However, it is Giddens's more recent writings on modernity that I use as a foundation for my discussion of mediated experience in this chapter. He defined modernity as particular modes of social organisation which emerged in Europe some three hundred to four hundred years ago and which are having an increasing impact right around the globe. As I pointed out in my introductory remarks in Chapter 1, Giddens was reluctant to accept – as many of his fellow commentators do – that we now live in a postmodern world. Instead, he has continued to argue that our present-day society is the outcome of a 'radicalising of modernity' (Giddens and Pierson 1998) – the rapid acceleration of institutional processes which have been evolving over a lengthy historical period – therefore referring to it as 'late' modern. For those of us in the field of media and cultural studies, I would suggest that the relevance of his observations on late modernity lies in the connections they make between such institutional processes and our routine experiences of everyday life. Of course, Giddens dealt only in passing with the significance of communication technologies because of the broad scope of his analysis, although it is my contention that the concepts he employed can provide a valuable framework within which to consider the role of modern electronic media.

## Disembedding/Re-Embedding

A concept of primary importance in Giddens's theory of modernity is that of time-space distanciation. This refers to a process in which social relations are lifted out of immediate interactional settings and stretched over potentially vast spans of global time-space – a dramatic 'disembedding' of social systems – but it is one that also involves a secondary, complementary moment of 're-embedding'. Here, those distanciated relationships are temporarily 'pinned down' to local conditions in new and distinctive types of face-to-face encounter. In the opening section of my chapter, I explain how he accounted for these twin moments in which social relations are disembedded and then re-embedded, before going on to apply his ideas in the following section on broadcasting and time-space distanciation.

For Giddens (1990: 16), modernity's dynamism 'derives from the separation of time and space'. People who lived in pre-modern cultures experienced time as connected to a sense of place. When was caught up with where, and with regular natural occurrences such as the changing of the seasons. Modernity, in stark contrast, is characterised by 'empty time' – uniformly measured by the mechanical clock and standardised across space with the adoption of international time-zoning and a common calendar (see Adam 1995). 'Everyone now follows the same dating system', wrote Giddens (1990:18), so that 'the approach of the "year 2000" ... is a global event'. In turn, this gives rise to a corresponding 'emptying of space', its dislocation from the particularities of local place:

> 'Place' is best conceptualised by means of the idea of locale, which refers to the physical settings of social activity as situated geographically. In pre-modern societies, space and place largely coincide, since the spatial dimensions of social life are, for most of the population, and in most respects, dominated by 'presence' – by localised activities. The advent of modernity increasingly tears space away from place by fostering relations between 'absent' others, locationally distant from any given situation of face-to-face interaction.
>
> (Giddens 1990: 18)

So in circumstances of time-space distanciation, our relationships with others are no longer confined to the locale. Furthermore, our day-to-day lives are touched to a greater extent by forces and happenings from far away. Places become phantasmagoric, 'thoroughly penetrated by and shaped in terms of social influences quite distant from them' (Giddens 1990: 19).

The lifting and stretching of social relations in the modern period has been facilitated by two main kinds of disembedding mechanism, which Giddens named symbolic tokens and expert systems. Discussing the former, his chosen example was the role of money as a token. In its fully developed form, 'money proper' – stored information as opposed to actual notes and coins – 'provides for the enactment of transactions between agents widely separated in time and space' (Giddens 1990: 24). The latter, meanwhile, were defined as 'systems of technical accomplishment or professional expertise that organise large areas of the material and social environment in which we live today' (Giddens 1990: 27). They are abstract systems of specialist knowledge that continually call on us to put our faith in the skills of absent others, making 'faceless commitments' as we do:

> Simply by sitting in my house, I am involved in an expert system, or a series of such systems, in which I place my reliance ... I know very little about the codes of knowledge used by the architect and the builder in the design and construction of the home, but I nonetheless have 'faith' in what they have done ... When I go out of the house and get into a car, I enter settings which are thoroughly permeated by expert knowledge – involving the design and construction of automobiles, highways, intersections, traffic lights and many other items ... When I park the car at the airport and board a plane, I enter other expert systems, of which my own technical knowledge is at best rudimentary.
>
> (Giddens 1990: 27–8)

However, there are also instances in modern daily living when lay individuals come into direct co-present contact with the human representatives of abstract systems – sharing the same physical location – and on such occasions, 'facework commitments' are combined with faceless ones of the sort described above. Trust in expert institutions can be developed at these 'access points', as long as the demeanour of system representatives is appropriate: 'the facework commitments which tie lay actors into trust relations ordinarily involve displays of manifest trustworthiness and integrity, coupled with an attitude of "business-as-usual", or unflappability' (Giddens 1990: 85).

Pursuing his earlier example of the plane journey, an activity that inevitably incorporates some element of risk or danger, Giddens (1990: 86) referred to 'the studied casualness and calm cheer of air crew personnel', which he suggested is 'probably as important in reassuring passengers as any number of announcements demonstrating statistically how safe air travel is'. As Arlie Hochschild's fascinating study of flight attendants has demonstrated, a sustained performance of this friendly professional demeanour over time – say on repeated long-haul flights – demands considerable 'emotional labour' on the part of the plane's cabin crew (Hochschild 1983). She was concerned to see things from the point of view of system representatives, whereas Giddens took an interest in the experience of passengers and in their relationships to an expert institution. He understood situated encounters of this type, conducted in the vivid immediacy of interpersonal interaction, as being central to the moment of re-embedding in which 'trust' is sought and 'risk' routinely negotiated.

An additional, regular feature of face-to-face engagements in late modern culture is the everyday practice of 'civil inattention', a concept borrowed by Giddens from sociologist Erving Goffman (1963). For instance, in contemporary urban life there are literally millions of occasions each day when otherwise absent strangers pass momentarily in a city street, briefly exchanging glances so as not to signal any hostile intent:

> Where the courtesy is performed between two persons passing on the street, civil inattention may take the special form of eyeing the other up to approximately eight feet ... and then casting the eyes down as the other passes – a kind of dimming of lights. In any case, we have here what is perhaps the slightest of interpersonal rituals, yet one that constantly regulates the social intercourse of persons in our society.
>
> (Goffman 1963: 84)

Of course, that special form of co-present communication between strangers is peculiar to modernity – 'a carefully monitored demonstration of what might be called polite estrangement' (Giddens 1990: 81) – and on the evidence of my summary of his work so far, it would not be hard to conclude that Giddens viewed the late modern world as a largely cold and impersonal one, save for the simulated friendliness of a few institutional representatives. His position is more subtle than this, though. In the course of mapping out a general phenomenology of modernity, he pointed to the quite complex intersections of intimacy and impersonality – of 'familiarity' and 'estrangement' – which are in play.

'Many aspects of life in local contexts continue to have a familiarity and ease to them, grounded in the day-to-day routines individuals follow', noted Giddens (1990: 140). Household and neighbourhood cultures, for example, can still offer their inhabitants some sense of symbolic warmth and security – even if, as I reported in Chapter 3 and Chapter 4, the lived reality of those places is not always entirely harmonious. Friendship networks, too, show little sign of waning in conditions of late modernity (Allan 1989b) – but, of particular importance for the analysis of broadcasting and time-space distanciation advanced below in my next section, I want to highlight Giddens's observation that familiarity and place are now less consistently connected than they were hitherto:

> This is less a phenomenon of estrangement from the local than one of integration with globalised 'communities' of shared experience ... We are all familiar with events, with actions, and with the visible appearance of physical settings thousands of miles away from where we happen to live. The coming of electronic media has undoubtedly accentuated these aspects of displacement, since they override presence so instantaneously and at such distance.
>
> (Giddens 1990: 141)

Here, in a fleeting reference to broadcasting, Giddens touched on the significance of communication technologies for what he later went on to call 'the mediation of experience' (see Giddens 1991). As this passage implies, instantaneous access to far-away places has contributed to a radical alteration in our experiences of space and time, of presence and absence. TV and radio provide technological means by which an 'intrusion of distant events into everyday consciousness' (Giddens 1991: 27) is possible. In addition, it is necessary for us to recognise that the consequences of such change for constructions of identity and community are likely to be considerable. Where we are no longer determines who we are – or who we are 'with' – to the same degree as it used to because electronically mediated communication has the potential to transform situation, interaction and identification.

While my application of Giddens's concepts in this chapter focuses on the part played by broadcasting in the disembedding and re-embedding of social life, these ideas about the mediation of experience – or else what his former colleague in sociology at Cambridge University, John Thompson (1994), has termed 'the transformation of interaction' – would be just as relevant to an analysis of other electronic media like computers and telephones. Indeed, in Chapter 8, I extend the discussion to include those technologies of mediated interpersonal communication – looking amongst other things at how their users present themselves to physically absent others in 'mediated encounters'.

## Broadcasting and Time-Space Distanciation

Clearly, then, television and radio have been involved in the disembedding or 'displacing' of social relationships – stretching communications across space and serving to create phantasmagoric places. Without leaving the privacy of the home, it is possible to 'witness' a public occasion at the same time as the people who are physically present at the spectacle. In fact, even when material has been pre-recorded, the virtual simultaneity of broadcast transmission and reception may still result in a mediated experience of liveness. Approaching TV from a phenomenological standpoint, Tony Wilson (1993: 35) identified what he named the medium's 'veridical effect': 'The electronic immediacy of the image asserts a closure between the spatio-temporal moment of a programme's discourse and the world of the viewer'. This is a mechanism by which the distances separating institutional production from domestic consumption can be bridged.

Although Wilson's book focuses on studio-based magazine shows and fictional programmes, we might look too at a form of output known as 'outside broadcasting'. Here, when watching a royal wedding or a World Cup soccer match while seated on the living-room sofa, there is sometimes a curious balance between feelings of presence and absence – of 'being there' and 'not being there'. So on the one hand, it is possible for us to have a strong sense of being transported to the occasion, seeing it unfold live before our eyes – but we are nevertheless conscious of occupying a household viewing context. Two communication theorists have even proposed that, with the advent of modern 'media events' which are quite deliberately designed for the cameras, not being there is now a 'ceremonial' experience in its own right:

> Members of the audience are radically separated from the ceremonial locus of the event and are also isolated from each other ... Attendance takes place in small groups congregated around the television set, concentrating on the symbolic centre, keenly aware that myriad other groups are doing likewise, in similar manner and at the same time. Ceremonial space has been reconstituted ... in the home ... the huge audience of media events has led to ... the domestic celebratory form.
>
> (Dayan and Katz 1992: 146)

In describing this domestic ceremony, the authors stressed that they did not consider it to be an 'impoverished' experience in comparison with actual attendance at the state or sporting event.

Rather, it involves a different mode of reception which has its own characteristic features. For instance, viewers at home who enjoy the benefit of multiple camera positions, action replays and commentaries often end up seeing and hearing more than those spectators gathered together in the crowd (Brown 1998).

This displacement, in which distant happenings permeate the lives of private consumers, is also bound up with what Giddens (1990) called 'the experience of risk' – to be understood in the broader context of what German social and political theorist Ulrich Beck (1992) has referred to as the emergence of a 'risk society'. Late modern culture, for Giddens, is marked by an increased awareness of the potentially dangerous aspects of social change. The time-space distanciation process gives rise to new connections between global developments and the localised settings of daily life, and these linkages may be extremely disturbing. A threat of large-scale military conflict or ecological disaster brings with it anxieties that most people 'bracket out' of conscious thought in order to get on with the practicalities of day-to-day living. Yet the experiences of millions of Europeans in the mid-1980s were profoundly touched by an accident in a nuclear power station at Chernobyl in the Soviet Union. Giddens pointed to these sorts of phenomenon as instances of the 'globalisation of risk', a growing number of events which have an environmental impact right around the planet. Television coverage of the Chernobyl catastrophe, along with weather reports of a wind from the east, understandably spread feelings of fear to viewers who were located thousands of miles away from the incident. That kind of media exposure could lead to trust in an expert system being diminished – but the precise balance between senses of security and danger depends partly on how risk is invested with significance in particular TV discourses and how different audiences, each bringing its own local knowledge and concerns to bear on the interpretation of audio-visual messages, perceive the hazards of nuclear energy. This is undoubtedly an area in which detailed qualitative research into practices of media representation and reception can help to provide a purchase on the varied cultural experiences of modernity (see Corner et al. 1990a; 1990b).

If broadcasting contributes to the moment of disembedding or displacement, then I want to propose that Giddens's concept of re-embedding is equally applicable in the analysis of mediated communication via television and radio, although in a way which he would not have anticipated. In his own discussion of the term, re-embedding was defined as 'the reappropriation or recasting of disembedded social relations so as to pin them down ... however partially or transitorily ... to local conditions of time and place' (Giddens 1990: 79–80). Trust in unknown others and abstract systems is routinely established through the civil inattention of passing strangers, and at the interface between expert institutions and lay individuals – between cabin crew and passengers on a plane or, to choose an alternative example, doctors in a consultation with their patients. On these social occasions, a degree of reassurance and even familiarity gets inserted into otherwise impersonal relationships. Without pushing Giddens's notion of re-embedding too far, my argument here is that we can fruitfully extend his notes on trust in co-present encounters so as to take account of the facework commitments made by media figures in their regular interactions with absent viewers and listeners – modes of address which incorporate a simulated, synthetic personalisation (Fairclough 1994). Despite the fact that there are few literally immediate situations of co-present meetings involving those personalities and their audiences, it is nevertheless possible for us to see the potential for a bond of intimacy (Horton and Wohl 1956) to be formed between them.

To assert that the electronic media frequently simulate co-presence with distant others, we need not accept the more problematic notions of 'simulation' and 'hyperreality' (Baudrillard 1988) which are circulating in postmodernist theory. Responding to Jean Baudrillard's grand claims on this matter, Giddens (1991: 27) acknowledged that 'in conditions of modernity ... the media do not mirror realities but in some part form them' – yet, he insisted, 'this does not mean ... the media have created an autonomous realm of "hyperreality" where the sign or image is everything'. Instead, as I have suggested in earlier chapters, the communicative styles of TV and radio are oriented to the everyday realities of viewers and listeners – and in appearing to address their talk and action directly to audiences in local settings of reception, broadcasting's personalities are engaged in the performance of a distinctively modern 'public drama' (see Chaney 1993). Constructing what Donald Horton and Richard Wohl (1956) once called a 'simulacrum of conversational give and take', they attempt to foster precisely those feelings of familiarity and trust which Giddens associated with re-embedding.

As Joshua Meyrowitz (1985: 122) has written: 'The evolution of media has begun to cloud the differences between stranger and friend and to weaken the distinction between people who are "here" and people who are "somewhere else"'. In developing his idea that audience members can form and maintain relationships with 'media friends', we could turn to the findings of empirical research carried out in the United States by Mark Levy (1982). He was concerned to chart viewers' responses to television news presentation:

> More than half of respondents agreed that newscasters are almost like friends one sees every day ... Few, if any, viewers confuse the newscasters with their actual friends, but many do relate to the broadcasters as something 'special' ... The para-social relationship develops over time and is based in part on a history of 'shared' experiences ... The daily visit of the news-caster is valued by the viewer, because the news persona, like a friend, brings 'gossip' in the form of news, or perhaps because the nightly appearance of the broadcaster provides a temporal benchmark for the day's activities.
>
> (Levy 1982: 180–1)

To assume that it is only the lonely, duped or undiscriminating consumer who identifies with presenters in this fashion would be wrong. Indeed, with the death of Brian Redhead – a respected broadcaster who had worked for many years on BBC Radio 4's early morning news programme – hundreds of listeners wrote letters to convey their deep sense of loss. Their mourning was caused by the absence of a known, familiar voice in the house or car, something which they had previously been able to 'count upon' and integrate into daily routines. Similar public expressions of loss followed the murder in 1999 of BBC TV newsreader and screen personality Jill Dando.

Meyrowitz (1985) asked whether such feelings should be under-stood as a 'new genre' of human grief, a kind of para-social grief. His examples of this late modern cultural phenomenon were reactions to the deaths of famous musical performers and politicians – John Lennon, Elvis Presley and John Kennedy – figures who were known to their dispersed fans or followers primarily through mediated experience rather than situated encounters. The sense of loss in these cases was sometimes felt as acutely as if it had been the death of a close personal friend or relative – and Meyrowitz himself acknowledged his 'strangely painful' response on hearing of Lennon's murder, having 'grown up with' him through the 1960s and 1970s via the artist's records, films and television performances.

## Issues of Difference and Inequality

Giddens's mapping of the 'contours' of late modernity is impressive. He advanced a model of contemporary society which managed to connect the domain of day-to-day lived experience with the institutional dynamics of social change – linking the 'intentionality' of personal dispositions with the 'extensionality' of globalising forces – and he rightly regarded shifts in the organisation of time, space and place as a fundamental feature of modern life. From our point of view in media and cultural studies, the lack of a fully developed analysis of electronically mediated communication in his writings may be compensated by the presence of ideas and insights that can now help us to develop one. However, I conclude my discussion of his work and its possible applications by pointing to certain dangers associated with Giddens's style of theorising – because I believe there are problems arising out of his tendency to speak about the experience of modernity in the singular, rather than highlighting a plurality of material circumstances and 'structures of feeling' in global culture.

He did recognise that modernity 'produces difference, exclusion and marginalisation', noting in passing the persistence of 'class divisions and other ... lines of inequality, such as those connected with gender or ethnicity', but he also admitted: 'I do not try to document those inequalities here' (Giddens 1991: 6). This is a pity, since his account of late modern living would be stronger still if it showed greater sensitivity to the diversity of positions which are occupied by different groups. Giddens is quite correct when asserting that, in many respects, we inhabit a single social world – and media technologies have made a significant contribution to the transnationalising process. Yet depending on exactly where 'we' are placed in relations of class, gender, generation and ethnicity – or in time-space geographies – there will be widely varying experiences of mediation and globalisation. Floya Anthias (1999) has offered a critique of Giddens's perspective on modern experience which takes a similar tack. There, she argued that:

> In much of his recent work Giddens deploys a universalising notion of 'we', related to modernity ... Giddens constructs a notion of the self ... who is historicised through the globalising tendencies of modernity ... The self is presented as unitary within these processes, thus downplaying issues of power and subordination within globalisation ... The person becomes reduced to the essentialised figure or self of ... modernity, which is identified with western social forms.
>
> (Anthias 1999: 156)

It follows, too, that experiences of local interaction will vary. So, returning again to practices of civil inattention which are performed by strangers in a city street, it is evident that such a routine encounter generates a higher level of anxiety for some than it does for others – depending upon who the participants are and precisely where the interaction happens. Dynamics of trust and risk in this localised situation are determined by the relative positions of the social subjects involved.

To be fair, Giddens is not the only theorist who might be accused of neglecting issues of difference and inequality when offering an account of contemporary globalisation. Despite its attention to shifts in the capitalist economic order, the postmodern geography of David Harvey (1989) – which was discussed briefly in my previous chapter – has been critically assessed by a fellow geographer, Doreen Massey (1992). Warning us not to get carried away with what she saw as the dizzy language of postmodernism, 'a special style of hype and hyperbole', she issued a note of caution and reminded her readers: 'Much of life for many people, even in ... the first world, still consists of waiting in a bus shelter with your shopping for a bus that never comes' (Massey 1992: 8). This is, she continued, hardly a 'graphic illustration of time-space compression'. The point was further emphasised in a recent commentary on Massey's piece:

> Globalisation is an uneven process, not just in that it involves 'winners and losers' or that it reproduces many familiar configurations of domination and subordination, but also in the sense that the cultural experience it distributes is highly complex and varied. It is important, then, not to mistake one narrow band of cultural experience for the whole of it, by becoming fascinated ... a particular temptation, as Massey hints, for academics ... with the technology and the associated lifestyle available to the 'information rich'.
>
> (Tomlinson 1999: 131)

Other criticism written in the same vein includes a feminist re-reading (Johnson 1993) of Marshall Berman's book on the experience of modernity (see Berman 1983) – in which the author insisted on specifying young women's relationships to cultural modernisation – and the work of Paul Gilroy (1993), who has attacked much of the current thinking on formations of modern society for its failure to articulate black people's particular experiences of social change. All of the critics cited here have realised, like Giddens, that there is a need to identify those historical upheavals which give shape and texture to daily life in the late modern era. Our challenge over the coming years is to construct a theory of modernity and its media that focuses not just on what subjects share, but also on the consequences of social divisions for everyday experience. This task, as my co-author and I propose in the next chapter, calls for empirical research which is sensitive to the local conditions and contradictions of global transformation.

# VII Identity, Tradition and Translation

KAREN QURESHI AND
SHAUN MOORES

Towards the end of Chapter 6, it was argued that there are problems associated with any theoretical work which attempts to deal with a singular 'experience of modernity'. Instead, so the argument went, it is important to recognise the 'uneven' distribution of cultural experiences in late modern society – and to try to explain something of their variety and complexity with reference to the plurality of positions that are occupied by different individuals and social groups. Even where theorists writing about globalisation have paid serious attention to questions of difference and social change – for example, Kevin Robins's notes on how 'forces of tradition' are being negotiated in contemporary practices of translation (Robins 1991), or James Clifford's reflections on the way in which particular identities are now a product of travel along specific migratory 'routes' rather than simply a matter of roots (Clifford 1997) – there is still a requirement to bring such ideas into contact with the findings of concrete empirical research carried out in local contexts. The aim of this chapter is to do precisely that.

We report on ethnographic field research which employed qualitative methods in looking at the lived experiences of a small group of Pakistani Scots in Edinburgh. This investigation represents the first stage of a larger, ongoing project that is concerned to explore how young, second-generation Pakistani Scots in the city are constructing their subjectivities. The following interpretative account is based on conversations and observations in private family homes and at several public functions, including Pakistan Day celebrations in the Scottish capital and a multicultural event called the 'Mela' – which is held at the end of the Edinburgh Festival, and regularly involves members of the city's Pakistani population. Fifteen young people aged between thirteen and twenty-five were interviewed in this initial study. Separate interviews with parents were also recorded during visits to households. To protect the anonymity of participants, their names have been altered or omitted. All of the parents had been born in that part of the Punjab which belongs to Pakistan and they had been resident in Britain for many years. Their children were all brought up in Scotland and are either in full-time education or else working in family businesses. Each of the fathers is a self-employed business man and the families are relatively secure in financial terms.

Back in the opening chapter of this book, when reference was made to Stuart Hall's discussion of what he had termed the presence of 'the Rest' in 'the West' (Hall 1992), remember that his main interest was in the emergence of cultures of hybridity and in the consequences these cultures might have for identity formation. It is the potential Hall saw for values and meanings to be 'translated' across social boundaries which interests us in the current chapter, and our chosen metaphor for practices of translation or hybrid-isation – one that was suggested by listening to the talk of the young people who participated in the research – is a type of popular music known as remix. Associated principally with the work of a British Asian producer, Bally Sagoo, remix is a musical form which combines Bombay film songs with a range of modern electronic rhythms (see Sharma et al. 1996). Sounds from 'the East' – inverted commas around the phrase signify our recognition that this category is a discursive construction, a product of Europe's imaginative geography (Said 1978) – are thereby translated or rerouted via the codes of Western youth cultures, which are themselves hybridised, and that collision of styles can symbolise broader patterns of change among the young women and men in Britain's South Asian diaspora. Shortly, we reflect on varying degrees of change which are now taking place, but let us begin by offering a few more general remarks on cultural identities in globalising processes.

## Investigating the Subjective Side of Social Change

A long-standing goal of research in cultural studies has been to investigate the subjective side of social change (Johnson 1986), those complex and varied types of identity, consciousness or lived experience which arise out of specific material conditions and historical transformations. In the present era, perhaps the most notable tendency is a move towards the global expansion of social networks. While globalisation is an old phenomenon, dating back at least as far as Europe's 'discovery' of 'other cultures' during the early modern period, its pace has quickened dramatically in the twentieth century with new developments in transportation and electronic communication. These technologies have figured in accelerating processes of time-space distanciation (Giddens 1990) and time-space compression (Harvey 1989), helping to stretch social relationships across vast geographical distances and to 'shrink the globe' by means of travel or mediated interaction.

One of the alleged consequences of globalisation is an increasing homogenisation of culture. In certain respects, then, it could be argued that the world has become a less diverse and almost 'placeless space' in which to live. From this perspective, local differences are seen to be gradually eroded over time as much the same range of products and services is consumed in various parts of the globe. Often bound up with related arguments concerning the impact of 'cultural imperialism' (see Tomlinson 1991), such a view is valuable in highlighting the power of the West over the Rest in the workings of the global economy – but what it fails to recognise, from another perspective, is the continuing plurality or hetero-geneity of many local cultures. Indeed, a recent commentator has suggested that the 'transnational connections' of globalisation may have made everyday life in particular urban settings far more complex than it previously was as a result of fresh cultural mixes and confluences (Hannerz 1996). So the significance of the local is not necessarily diminished by the large-scale processes of the global. Analysing the micro-worlds of modern daily living can actually serve to illuminate those processes at the point where they permeate local cultures, as they are 'articulated' in – connected with and expressed through – routine social practices.

Beyond both the global and local dimensions of contemporary social change, there lies what Hall (1997) has recently called 'the final frontier', the realm of subjectivity. This is the domain of 'inner life', of selfhood and personal experience. For those working in media and cultural studies, there has always been a recognition of the socially constructed character of subjectivity. Adopting an anti-essentialist stance, theorists and researchers have insisted upon explaining identity formation with reference to objective social arrangements – and have sometimes sought to investigate the collec-tive representations and narratives through which individuals position or locate themselves as, for example, national subjects (see Formations Collective 1984; Bhabha 1990). However, with new global and local transformations – intensified patterns of migration across frontiers in the latter half of the twentieth century, the transnational flow of mediated sounds and images, and the 'relocation' of popu-lations and signs in different cultural contexts – come further chal-lenges for work on subjectivity and social change. In particular, we would argue that there is a need for empirical case studies which consider the 'double consciousness' (Gilroy 1993) of peoples who inhabit plural or multiple cultures – who speak at least two 'languages', in the broadest sense of the term, and who must 'translate' between them in order to fashion their self and group identities.

This research on the experiences of young Pakistani Scots in Edinburgh is designed to generate material of just that sort, although we are clearly not alone in exploring the changing contours of youth and ethnic identities in British urban settings. A number of ethnographic projects, all carried out in England during the late 1980s or early 1990s, have charted similar territory. For instance, Claire Alexander (1996) discussed the dynamic negotiation of 'Black British' subjectivities, basing her account on in-depth observations of two groups of young people in London – mainly of African-Caribbean origin – with whom she socialised and spoke at length about senses of home, community and nationhood. Her fieldwork also foregrounded gender relations and detailed the social construction of black masculinities. Meanwhile, sociologist Les Back (1996) has written on the expressive cultures of modern black and South Asian music in Britain. He described the technological forms of sound system performance and 'bhangra beat', and his commentary pointed to the emergence of a new 'cultural intermezzo' in the space of exchange between different musical styles. Finally, Marie Gillespie (1995) – in a book which helped to inspire the planning of this study – considered the lived experiences of young Punjabi Londoners in Southall. Focusing on their everyday talk about TV and video texts such as soap operas, advertisements and Bombay films, she painted a vibrant picture of the ongoing translation or 'crossover' between cultures. In our view, a specific strength of Gillespie's work was her constant reference to the words of informants in the field. We try to do the same in what follows, frequently quoting the voices of interviewees to provide a foundation for the analysis.

## Conventional Values in Private and Public Settings

As a way into examining the views of the young Pakistani Scots featured in this study, we want to outline the values and practices of their parents who migrated from South Asia to North-West Europe, since it is necessary to understand the powerful conservative forces which can operate both in the household and in wider social contexts. Central to the conventional value system is a series of related ideas that have to do with family unity, religious faith, respect and honour – and it is those cultural values which give rise to certain hopes and fears for children who are making the difficult transition through youth to adulthood. It is also against this back-drop that the young women and men must fashion identities and cultures of their own, actively negotiating the power of convention.

The significance of family unity became clear during observation time spent at the homes of interviewees. All of the parents believed the maintenance of extended family relationships to be important, even if it meant overcoming the problems of physical separation. For instance, the telephone is used for 'kinkeeping' purposes (Moyal 1989) – for staying in touch with relatives in Pakistan or elsewhere in Britain – and a degree of financial security among these families enables them to travel 'back home' occasionally, or invite relatives to holiday in Scotland. In addition, much like the Southall Punjabi households discussed by Gillespie (1995), intimate links with kin living at a distance are sustained through the exchange of amateur videos – usually recordings of wedding cele-brations. Indeed, on a visit to one family, an inquiry concerning the traditional marriage ceremony led to a screening of the wedding video sent by the father's cousin from Fiaslabad.

When parents were asked what particular values they are seeking to pass on to their children, adherence to the Islamic religion and a respect for adults were those cited most often. This mother's reply is typical:

> My faith and my culture ... like respecting the older gener-ation and always doing this in the future ... When my daughters will get married respect your in-laws, you know, and teach your children about your culture ... Try to respect the views of marriage, you know. When we choose partners for them, hopefully they will understand.

That desire to reproduce conventional values is accompanied by fears about what are regarded as the potentially 'corrupting' or 'corrosive' influences of Western society (Ballard 1982). In the following quotation, a father points to some of them and acknow-ledges the difficulty that different sets of expectations could cause his son:

> When he is in school, he has to act as everybody else does but ... his friends will be going to discos and to girlfriends, and this and that ... he knows he will not be expected to do all this ... So there is a lot of pressure on the children.

Perhaps in an effort to counter the perceived dangers of public life outside the home, parents in this study – like a couple of those featured in Chapter 4 – have invested in a wide range of communication and information technologies for consumption and use in the private sphere. For example, the children in one of the domestic settings which was observed have a bedroom each with their own television set, video recorder and personal computer. Yet the position of the media in these households is complex and contradictory. Their purchase may be designed to make the home a more attractive place for young people – to offer pleasures which compete with those available beyond the front door – but a technology like TV bridges boundaries between the public and the private, bringing in representations that parents can find disturbing or distasteful:

> Even before nine o'clock, there are some programmes I find something's happening. They are very disturbing ... I mean *EastEnders* and *Neighbours* and *Brookside* ... promoting homosexuality and lesbianism ... The last one that I saw was very distasteful ... the *Brookside* a few weeks ago, a brother was sleeping with a sister. In our culture that is something that was never heard of.

Given the presence of at least two television sets in all the households visited, there are opportunities for children to watch separately from parents, and this is generally the preferred mode of viewing among the young people who were interviewed. In part, their preference has to do with differences of programme taste, but it is evidently bound up with the embarrassment and discomfort they feel as a result of parental disapproval of British TV content.

An amusing exchange, involving three sisters and their friend, serves to illustrate that experience of discomfort and reveals knowing techniques for self-censorship. The girls are talking here about viewing situations in which the sisters' parents are sitting in the same room as they watch the screen:

> *Fatima*: There are scenes when you will automatically turn the channel.
> *Salma*: It is so funny because if you have the remote control in your hand ...
> *Fatima*: And you haven't changed it ...
> *Farhat*: They [parents] will give you weird looks. They will just turn round and ... give you like a weird look.
> *Salma*: Like if I'm watching a film or something on television and I feel a dirty scene is coming up, just before it happens, 'I'm going to bed'.
> *Fatima*: Then you come back in, 'who wants tea?'

*Soraya*: That's like me the day we were watching something and I wasn't paying attention. I think I was biting my nail or something and they [sisters] were all going 'change the channel', and I went 'what?' Then I turned round and they were totally shouting at me, 'change the channel'.

*Salma*: Then by the time you change it back, it is like three scenes have gone past or something (laughter).

Salma also reported that when she tries to watch *Neighbours* in the living room, her mother – who disapproves of the programme – will ask her to vacuum the carpets. Along with the sort of 'weird looks' from parents described by Farhat, this is a way of expressing disapproval without having to enter directly into discussion with children on topics which are felt to be sensitive. As Javed, one of the boys in the study, said: 'They never talk about drink, drugs, sex ... they never talk about these things'.

Outside the domestic arena, too, there are pressures on young people to conform to certain standards of morality and behaviour. This can best be illustrated with reference to the notion of 'izzit', which has considerable significance for South Asians. The meanings of izzit are bound up with issues of family honour, or with an individual's public standing in 'the community', and that honour or standing is particularly vulnerable to the impact of gossip (see Gillespie 1993). Given the relatively small size of Edinburgh's Pakistani population, most people know each other – through attendance at the city's four mosques or through membership of various associations, societies and sports clubs. So the lives of these young Pakistani Scots are influenced, to differing extents, by the threat of harmful talk. Although parents do not always consider a specific restriction upon their children to be necessary, they still enforce it selectively because of a fear that the family's reputation will be damaged. One girl pointed out the kind of contradiction which can arise as a consequence of this fear. She explained that, whilst her parents allow her to go to the city sports stadium at Meadowbank, she is not permitted to watch local cricket matches where Pakistani men are playing – precisely because it would risk unfavourable gossip.

Indeed, izzit is more dependent on the behaviour of female family members than that of males, and this may have an important bearing on the marriage prospects of daughters (Afshar 1989). The social impact of gossip is therefore felt most deeply by girls. Those interviewed in this study were conscious of, and in some instances frustrated by, the gender imbalance. The following conversation with one of the sisters quoted above and her boy cousin, Bashir, took place soon after the Mela:

> *KQ*: Did you go to that concert on Saturday with Jazzy B [Canadian Asian 'bhangra' singer]?
>
> *Salma*: Mm. I enjoyed that like, you know, I like a bit of bhangra. I was just dying to get off my seat.
>
> *KQ*: And did you?
>
> *Salma*: No! Did you want my mum and dad to kill me?
>
> *KQ*: But the boys do it.
>
> *Salma*: Yeah.
>
> *Bashir*: The girls were doing it as well.
>
> *KQ*: So some of the girls were dancing?
>
> *Salma*: Yeah, the ones from Glasgow.
>
> *KQ*: Those of you who felt restrained, and weren't able to get up and dance, what did you do?
>
> *Salma*: We just clapped ... in our seat and went [gesture of frustration].

What she implies here is that the relative anonymity of the Glasgow girls in Edinburgh freed them from the danger of gossip reaching their parents. The safest opportunities for young women to dance locally are during wedding 'mhendi' celebrations, which are traditionally held in 'purdah' (see Werbner 1996) – but even in these seemingly private circumstances, modern media technology has made dancing risky as such events are now filmed for wider public consumption: 'It goes into ... a wedding video, and then it goes out ... everybody wants to see it ... and they say "Oh, their girl is dancing, tut tut"'.

## Gender, Generation and Interpersonal Relationships

In this section of the chapter, we explore further the gendered and generational dynamics of lived experience. First, this is done by mapping the everyday practices of girls who inhabit plural and potentially contradictory cultural domains, and who are creating their senses of personal and collective identity within multiple constraints. Secondly, attention is paid to those techniques of self-presentation that are employed by the boys interviewed and observed in the study. Our main concern there is with constructions of style, and with the making of identifications and distinctions. Any differences of emphasis in our discussion of these young Pakistani-Scottish women and men are indicative of a disparity in their own experiences or interests. Thirdly, and lastly here, we turn to address the changing attitudes surrounding arranged wedding matches – known as 'rishtas' – and the emergence of so-called 'love marriages'.

### Girls: Living Across Two Worlds

So young British Asians can find themselves confronting different sets of cultural values with often contradictory expectations. However, as our preceding commentary suggests, the demands upon women within certain interpretations of Islam might make any translation across those value systems especially difficult for second-generation girls (see Afshar 1994). The young women featured in the study spoke about various ways of dealing with this dichotomy in their lives. A range of emotional responses was recorded, and we begin with an expression of resignation and guilt:

> *Nazreen*: These days in Edinburgh, most girls go out and all that, most girls do … I know in our religion you are not supposed to, but we can't really help it now because we are mixed up with Scottish girls as well, and they like going out.
> *KQ*: Do you feel comfortable with that?
> *Nazreen*: In a way.
> *KQ*: In a way do you not feel comfortable with it?
> *Nazreen*: Because you think about your religion afterwards, 'Oh, we've been out'.

Other mixed expressions of cultural identity were related to the girls' talk about clothes. Most of the young women feel positively about traditional dress – which is routinely worn at home or at Pakistani functions, and typically takes the form of 'shelvar kemis', a long shirt hanging over loose-fitting trousers. For instance, Aziza proudly stated that were she at an event with 'a thousand people there and nobody wearing traditional clothes … I could walk in … and I would wear it'. Similarly, great pleasure was taken by some of the interviewees on seeing images of Princess Diana wearing shelvar kemis during a visit to Pakistan shortly before her death. This was read as a welcome validation of their own look. At the same time, though, one girl drew the line at being made by parents to wear traditional dress in particular educational contexts because she wanted to fit in with her fellow Scottish students: 'I had to wear Asian clothes when I was at school … but when I got to … college, that is where I really had to start putting my foot down … it was difficult'. Below, two of the young women explain how a change of outfit – on arriving home from school – symbolised their shifting and plural subjectivities:

> *Salma*: When I went to school I was ... somebody totally
> different, and when I came home I was totally different. I
> would like change my clothes. I just felt like, 'I'm living
> two lives'.
> *Fatima*: Yeah, like you would go out ... you'd skive, you'd
> have a laugh, you'd muck about with your friends ... do all
> the things that if your parents ever heard they would go
> mad, then you would come home and ... you would be the
> good little daughter or something.

We could say, then, that each style of clothing involved 'putting
on' a different feminine identity and performing the appropriate
role. Their presentation of gendered self was therefore dependent
upon the interactional settings in which they found themselves, and
on what Erving Goffman (1963) would have termed the different
'situational proprieties'.

Inside the classroom, it is talk about television soap operas which
creates much of the common ground for sociable interactions with
non-Asian schoolfriends, offering the girls an opportunity to engage
in a sort of cultural crossover. The plots and characters from
programmes such as *Neighbours* and *Home and Away* provide them
with a shared resource for the discussion of topical issues. This
enables the young women to demonstrate their TV viewing competences – the 'generic', 'serial-specific', and more general 'cultural'
knowledges (Brunsdon 1981) which they have developed as avid
soap followers: 'We always talk about what happened in *Neighbours*
yesterday, because there is always someone on our table that misses
it, so we have to fill them in'.

Having said that, these interviewees also acknowledged difficulties in sustaining friendships with their white peers, particularly
once they reach the late teens. Earlier, Nazreen spoke about the
inevitability of mixing and socialising with 'Scottish girls', yet the
chances to do so are nevertheless limited by some restrictions on the
movement of young women. Aziza, for example, goes out with her
white friends 'now and again' – but she is 'not allowed to go to
night clubs and things like that', nor does she necessarily want to
go. To quote another instance, Seema compared her own position
with that of non-Asian girls at the school which she attends:

> They can go to discos and stuff. There is a disco at the end of
> term in our school ... the Asians don't go to it and they do.
> Sometimes that's how you kind of partner up ... whether you
> want to talk about ... 'I'll pick you up and we will go
> together', and you can't exactly join in.

When girls do go out, there may be a need to be secretive about what happens outside the family home. One told the story of how she managed to persuade her parents to let her go to a sixth-year school leavers' dance by giving them the impression it was a formal dinner. Meanwhile, others recounted how they would pretend to be shopping when they were actually watching a film at the cinema. In fact, Nazreen herself admitted that while she and her mates might 'muck around with boys', they still 'have to be careful that no other Pakistani will see us'.

Given those constraints, young Pakistani-Scottish women spend a good deal of their leisure time within the private sphere, with the telephone frequently being used to combat any experiences of domestic isolation. This was evident on visits to households and during interviews when girls left the room to take incoming calls, chatting excitedly to friends. It has been noted elsewhere, by anthropologist Pnina Werbner (1988), that British Asian women tend to develop strong friendship networks of their own – and here the medium is being employed to create a social space for the intimate exchange of information and narratives. Its use provides an important source of support and personal enjoyment, as reflected in the words of an interviewee who declared: 'The phone, it's my life'.

It is important for us to qualify this by adding that three of the older girls in the study have recently built on their friendship links, helping to found a new young women's group which attempts to give a greater public presence to second-generation Muslim girls in Edinburgh. As Fatima explained: 'We just want to do things that young women would be interested in, like educational things, all different activities like sports'. This group has so far organised workshop discussions, taken up charitable causes and contributed to Women's International Day celebrations in the city. Interestingly, Aziza justified involvement in those celebrations in terms of teaching non-Asian women about their own distinctive experiences:

> To give information to the Scottish people around us, to make them more aware of our culture. For a lot of the Scottish people ... our culture is alien ... and I think it is better for them to know, because it just makes them more familiar with us. It is just like a kind of friendly bond because, you know, we are going to stay here. We may as well make it comfortable for ourselves.

Her account makes it clear that, while the group may in some ways be presenting a collective female challenge to the values of their parents' generation – their efforts have met with cynicism from certain Pakistani Scots within the city – in other ways it is intended to promote a pride in, and an awareness of, conventional cultural practices. The choice of positional terms like 'us', 'them' and 'our' also indicates a continuing sense of social difference or distance from 'Scottish people'.

## Boys: On Style, Identification and Distinction

In the case of the young men, too, it became clear that clothing – along with other aspects of style and fashion – plays a significant part in their constructions of identity and difference. The image of youthful masculinity which they put on display is the product of a symbolic creativity (Willis 1990), an inventive borrowing and 'remixing' of cultural signs from West and East, although we would want to argue that the precise form of this translation or 'hybridisation' requires careful examination because it involves them making a number of structured identifications and taste distinctions in their consumption and leisure activities.

Gillespie (1995), in her work on Punjabi youths in Southall, observed a 'selective appropriation' of black styles – and similar practices were noted in the Edinburgh study. It is chiefly to black North American culture that the boys who were interviewed are looking for their points of identification with Western society, rather than to the dominant tastes of white British youth:

> *Javed*: I think most Asians, like, they've kind of got their own style.
> *KQ*: Tell me about it.
> *Manzoor*: We are always wearing baggy kind of stuff.
> *Javed*: Like ... you wouldn't catch many Asians wearing tight jeans ... That's not their sort of style, we're more like kind of Afro-American style.

This identification is available via the media of music and film. For example, Bashir likes listening to 'house' dance tracks and cites his favourite cinema stars as Denzel Washington and Will Smith. The latter's lead role in a recent Hollywood blockbuster, *Independence Day*, ensured the film's popularity among these young Pakistani-Scottish men. Manzoor explains how 'Asians like us tend to go for more ... black movies'. At the Mela celebrations, it was possible to read the boys' postures and gestures of camaraderie as rooted in popular representations of African-American youth, embodying a cool self-confidence and including palm-slapping greetings.

An additional element of male fashion is the display of jewellery.

One of the boys showed off a gold chain he was wearing around his neck: 'Every Asian has got that from Pakistan, like rings ... everyone does have a chain, a nice watch, things like that'. It is worth mentioning here that on the cover of a Bally Sagoo CD – *Rising From the East* – the British Asian performer and music producer is pictured wearing an earring, two necklaces and several rings on each hand. Indeed, his remix sound serves to symbolise the cultural borrowings of the young men who listen to him – juxtaposing various black musical styles like 'electro', rap and reggae with Eastern instruments and vocals.

Technologies of transportation and electronic communication also play a crucial part in this cross-cultural 'bricolage' (Hebdige 1979). Javed spoke about the importance of possessing, or aspiring to possess, a car and a mobile telephone with which to 'pose' – and when asked who the boys were posing for, he replied:

> Mostly girls ... each other as well, like you'll get recognised by your car ... it's like pride, respect ... izzit. It's like keeping your respect up, sort of thing. People kind of look up to you.

Salma confirmed this, commenting that 'it's mostly the boys ... that have all got mobile phones ... just as they turn eighteen or sixteen, they get a mobile phone'. The value of these gadgets appears to be largely symbolic, since they signify entry into a particular group identity and culture, although one of the interviewees admitted that he and his girlfriend are secretly conducting a romantic relationship using mobile telephones.

If this articulation of identity involves an appropriation of and an identification with black styles, then equally it depends upon practices of distinction (see Bourdieu 1984) and senses of difference from certain white youth cultures: 'Like rave music, we're not into that ... They're not into jewellery and everything ... Or like football, we're not into football'. Those sports that were preferred to soccer included the martial arts and cricket, at which the touring Pakistan team had recently beaten Scotland in a one-day friendly international played at Stockbridge in Edinburgh. However, Bashir told of how his interest in playing rugby had led to him being called a 'coconut' by some other young Pakistani Scots. He explained that the insult arises when 'you're Asian ... your skin colour is dark, and you act white ... anyway, you don't do things you are supposed to'.

Compared with the girls whose voices were heard in the previous subsection of our chapter, the boys who participated in the research appear to be less restricted in their movements – leading some of the young women to talk of double standards – but there is still a parental monitoring of how and where sons spend their leisure time. One boy described the way in which he gets around this:

> *Manzoor*: I just sneak out.
> KQ: What do you mean, sneak out? Do you mean go out when they think you're in?
> *Manzoor*: Yeah ... I don't say anything, I just walk out. That's what I usually do.

Yet outside the place of the home, such resistance to authority can lead to a reproduction of sexist values. For example, young men may engage in urban gossip about particular girls – calling their behaviour or reputation into question: 'You get any guy and say to him, "What Asian girl goes out?", and they will give you the same names ... because there is a few girls who go about with guys'. The collective name given to these young women within masculine youth culture is 'awara' girls – a derogatory term which means 'always out'.

### Arranged Matches and Love Marriages

Having outlined the gendered identities and lived experiences of these young Pakistani Scots, we now look at issues of marriage and romance. For many South Asians, marriage is perceived principally as an alliance between two families and as a consequence the marital happiness of the couple is considered to be of lesser significance. Haleh Afshar (1994) noted that a match is arranged by kin with what are seen as the 'best interests' of the next generation in mind. While the young people interviewed in this study did not express a desire to abandon the arranged marriage system completely, several were looking for a greater say in those arrangements. One of the girls, Nazreen, described a school project which she had written on the subject of arranged marriages. This had entailed her talking to different groups of people about their views on the matter:

> I just wrote about what the youngsters thought about it and what the elders thought about it. The elders thought arranged marriages, yes ... my mum's age and dad's age, they agreed ... The ones my age, they thought they would like arranged marriages but they wouldn't like it a proper one. They would like to meet the person before.

Dissatisfaction with matches where the couple do not get to know each other first is articulated below, as a friend's 'post-nuptial courtship' is discussed:

*Salma*: My friend, she got married ... he's in London, she's in Edinburgh. She's not going till the wedding reception happens. I spoke to him on the phone and I was saying, 'you know I can guarantee you'll be happy with Nazim'. I was just joking around, and I'm saying 'Nazim is such a nice person'.

*Bashir*: So he doesn't already know that before he gets married.

*Salma*: She said to me after we got off the phone, 'you know I could live with him and he might think I'm horrible'. I just thought, you've just got married to someone that you don't know properly. Okay, she knows his favourite colour is black, and basically the questions she was asking him on the phone ... I was sitting next to her, 'don't you like Asian music?' ... it was like, you are married to him and you are asking questions like Asian music, and 'what kind of clothes do you wear?'

*Bashir*: Things that you should already know ... it's kind of stupid.

A potential solution to the problem perceived by Salma and Bashir involves a compromise between the conventional system of arranged marriages and Western ideas of romantic love – although it would be a mistake for us to conclude that discourses of love and romance are an exclusively Western phenomenon, since there are highly sentimental themes which run through old Bombay film songs and narratives. This compromise is what the young people here called a 'love marriage' – a match that still gets organised, on the face of it, by parents for the couple. However, it arises when the girl and boy have courted secretly and have managed either to persuade or manipulate parents into arranging their wedding match for them – a 'self-arranged marriage', as one interviewee put it. It can also be the result of a parent finding out about their secret relationship. For instance, a father who discovered his son had a girlfriend told him to stop seeing her until schooling was completed, promising to approach the girl's family at that point to ask for a rishta.

Among British Asians, there has long been a trend towards living in 'conjugal' rather than 'extended family' households (see Ballard 1982), but some of the girls' anxieties about marriage centre on the possibility of having to reside under the same roof as in-laws. Leaving the parental home may effectively mean exchanging one set of domestic constraints for another. Fatima explained: 'A lot of times ... the husband's family is the problem ... It is all tradition again ... like they have to know what you are doing or where you are going'. Yet if escape from an unsatisfactory match is difficult, it is no longer impossible. Alongside the move towards love marriages, there is now a growing number of divorces: 'In Pakistan, they sort of live with it. Here, because they know about divorce ... the marriage can be annulled ... even if they have kids'.

## The Consumption of Mediated Symbolic Goods

Throughout the present chapter, while discussing processes which have been termed tradition and translation, we have made passing reference to the creative consumption of symbolic goods like TV and music – and in this final section, the social significance of these mediated forms is foregrounded. Of specific interest here is the fact that all of the households visited have access to 'Asian' programming through satellite or cable television services. All but one had installed a satellite dish to enable them to receive Zee UK and Europe – a new subsidiary channel of Zee Asia, with a potential audience of two million Asian viewers in Britain and a further eight million across mainland Europe (Sreberny-Mohammadi 1996) – with the remaining family subscribing to cable in order to watch the Asia Net channel.

For parents, these services provide a routine and familiar point of contact with their 'cultural heritage'. Zee, for example, is dominated by content which offers older viewers a nostalgic link with the past (see Gillespie 1989) and an imaginative experience of travelling back home:

> Sometimes I feel like a salmon, you know, I want to go up stream to my origins and I think part of that fantasy is Zee TV. You are fantasising, you are thinking you are back home, you are seeing your culture.

So the transnational territories of transmission (Rath 1985) made available by satellite TV are resonating with the memories and fantasies of first-generation Pakistani Scots. The majority of Zee's programmes can be described as light entertainment and drama, and many of those reflect the immense popularity of 'Bollywood' cinema. As well as screening the films themselves, this station broadcasts several movie quiz shows and programmes featuring interviews with – and gossip about – the film stars, directors and producers. It also transmits Pakistani dramas that are considered by the parents in this study to be of high quality and educational value. The only area of broadcast output where they preferred to watch British or local 'Scottish' television is the news, because it is seen as more reliable and relevant to their day-to-day concerns.

In contrast, younger viewers expressed a general preference for programmes shown on British terrestrial TV. These include the Australian soap operas mentioned earlier in the chapter, along with cult American series such as *The X Files* and *Friends*. Additionally, all the boys said that they liked *Top Gear*, reflecting their keen interest in cars. However, Zee is now recognising the existence of new, second- and third-generation audiences – making its own 'lifestyle' and children's shows in Britain. One of these, entitled *Your Zindgi*, broadcast material which was filmed at the Edinburgh Mela. This contained a sequence in which an interviewee, Rashida, formed part of a group chanting the programme's jingle. There was considerable excitement the following week as she tuned in to watch the screen performance with her sister, Rahmat, and friends. Another interviewee, Javed, spoke about his enjoyment of listening to a particular presenter on Zee. He talked about his identification with the presenter's playful 'code switching' or 'crossing' (Rampton 1995) between different languages:

> It's a kids' programme but it's really funny to watch. It's a guy sitting there, and he's just talking in Urdu and then he changes to English ... like us lot if we were sort of talking amongst each other, we wouldn't be talking pure English. We would be talking English and Urdu and Punjabi, sort of everything mixed, you know. That is what he does.

This inventive crossing or mixing of sounds in conversational discourse might be understood as the linguistic equivalent of remix music, or of various 'British bhangra' styles.

Musical cultures are fertile grounds for the cultivation of self and collective identities (Frith 1996), and in this research it became clear from the start that the consumption of music was an important element in everyday experiences of social change among these young Pakistani Scots. Despite a feeling that the music scene is 'happening' somewhere else, over in Glasgow or down in England, the young women and men are enthusiastic about recent developments in British Asian dance sounds. The sentimental Bombay film songs which appeal to parents – in one household, there were more than a hundred cassette recordings on display in the living room – have been translated into a contemporary style for the youth market. Again, Javed explained:

> I suppose it is funny. I mean, being brought up here and everything ... but we listen to film songs. You know, that's

what we're all into, lovey-dovey stuff. They're normal Indian film songs, but they just mix in a few beats, make it modern … change the words around.

Bhangra, too, a traditional form of folk music with its origins in the Punjab, has been 're-invented' (Back 1996) in the British context – resulting in hybrid rhythms known as 'house bhangra' and 'bhangra beat', which incorporate sound sampling, drum machines and synthesisers.

# VIII The Dynamics and Consequences of Mediated Interaction

In this concluding chapter, my concern is to delimit a distinctive object of inquiry which I propose to name 'the mediated interaction order'. Under that general heading, I try to pull together a number of themes and issues which run through the book, whilst also pushing my analysis and arguments a stage further. Naming the object in this way, I am making an intentional reference to the title of a paper written by Erving Goffman (1983) shortly before his death. For Goffman, the interaction order was understood primarily as a realm of face-to-face interpersonal contact: 'that which uniquely transpires in social situations ... environments in which two or more individuals are physically in one another's response presence' (Goffman 1983: 2). Throughout his career in sociology, he argued for the face-to-face realm to be taken seriously as a focus of inquiry. It was, he believed, the site of 'a particular kind of activity as in the phrase "the economic order"' – but it was also apparent to him that 'as an order of activity, the interaction one, more than any other perhaps, is in fact orderly' (Goffman 1983: 5). Late in his academic life, he did begin to explore some features of communication at a distance via the electronic media – for example, in an essay which he published on radio talk (see Goffman 1981) – yet that was never his main analytical interest. My question here is whether it might be possible to conceive of a mediated interaction order with its own particular conventions and organising principles.

Of course, it could be said that all social interaction – including that which takes place between co-present participants – is 'mediated by' the signs of language or gesture. However, this chapter deals specifically with various forms of electronically mediated communication between absent others, or else with those situated interactions in which the media play a crucial part. That covers relations between performers and audiences in broadcasting, communication via telephone and computer networks, and routine negotiations involving the use of electronic media in everyday life.

While there is much existing work to be found in these separate areas – my chapter reviews selected examples drawn from the literature – it is still unusual, even in a media and cultural studies context, for such technologies and types of communication to be grouped together in a single domain of investigation. A traditional boundary between the categories of mass and interpersonal communication has tended to obstruct its formation, despite a few notable efforts to transcend the division (see Gumpert and Cathcart 1982; Meyrowitz 1985). By assembling ideas and findings from a range of writings, I want to put forward a case for the convergence of this theory and research around a shared interest in the dynamics and consequences of mediated interaction in modern society. The chapter, and with it the book, ends by asking how new work on the media's significance can now be developed.

## Central Analytical Themes

As a prelude to the discussion that follows, I begin by highlighting the three central analytical themes which permeate subsequent sections of this chapter. Since the current section serves in part to 'crystallise' key points made elsewhere in the book, my summary of these themes needs only to be brief. The first issue here has to do with the position of electronic media in the spatial and temporal organisation of social life. Television, radio, telephones and computers are communication technologies that have contributed to a shift in arrangements of space and time. Alongside other technological systems and institutional mechanisms in the modern world, they have lifted social relations out of face-to-face contexts and stretched or extended them across large distances, dislocating space from place in the process. For instance, we have seen how an event which occurs on the other side of the globe can be witnessed in live time 'as it happens'. It is possible, too, for us to engage in dialogue of different kinds with distant interlocutors. Consequently, the character of place is radically altered as our everyday settings or locales are touched by remote influences and contacts.

A second theme revisited in the following discussion is cultural experiences of modernity. This relates to the issue of how it feels to live day-to-day in contemporary conditions – and, more particularly, what difference communication technologies have made to the nature of routine social experience. In modern society, for example, patterns of familiarity and estrangement have changed quite dramatically. Although we may enjoy a relationship of intimacy at a distance with a TV personality or fellow Internet user, some of our daily contacts in urban settings can be with people who are completely unknown to us, the impersonal sea of faces through which we pass on a city street. Presence and absence are themselves experienced in new ways as our opportunities for instantaneous access to distant and 'virtual' locations are increased.

My third major theme is the role of electronically mediated communication in constructions of self-identity and community. With the spatial and temporal changes outlined above, that lifting and stretching of human relationships, comes a rapid expansion in the 'stock' of symbolic resources which is available to social subjects as they actively shape their individual and collective identities. If the self is best understood as the product of an ongoing 'autobiographical narrative', then we need to investigate where the 'raw material' for our personal stories is obtained, and to what extent those resources are extracted from the flow of mediated interactions. Similarly, it is important for us to remember that modern communities are imaginative constructs, fictions manufactured at the point where private lives and public discourses intersect. As I have observed previously, senses of community are now less place-bound than they used to be.

## TV and Radio: Mediated Quasi-Interaction

Let us consider once more the case of broadcasting and examine the type of communication which John Thompson (1995) has called 'mediated quasi-interaction'. He employed a prefix to signal the fact that, although performers and audiences in television or radio are 'linked together in a process of ... symbolic exchange', relations between them will not be characterised by 'the degree of reciprocity and interpersonal specificity of other forms of interaction' (Thompson 1995: 84). In other words, because of a separation between the place of cultural production and multiple contexts of consumption, broadcast communication is typically 'monological' rather than 'dialogical' – there is a one-way centralised transmission of messages to geographically dispersed groups of viewers and listeners. Nevertheless, partly as a result of their distance from the message producers, those consumers may be able to exercise a degree of choice and 'interpretative agency' in their engagements with TV and radio – and because the moments of transmission and reception in broadcasting are virtually simultaneous, viewers and listeners can experience some of the feelings of immediacy that have traditionally accompanied face-to-face encounters. This is a phenomenon which was originally observed in the United States during the

1950s by Donald Horton and Richard Wohl (1956). Thompson's concept of mediated quasi-interaction clearly echoes their notion of para-social interaction, which they used to describe the taken-for-granted yet remarkable relationship that the various personalities of television and radio conduct with their absent addressees. So even though the media figure in the studio is actually communicating with a scattered audience of strangers, regular viewers or listeners may form ties of emotional intimacy – across space and over time – with a persona they feel they have come to know.

We need not see such emotional attachments as pathological. Indeed, while they are quite remarkable, it could be argued that they are a perfectly normal outcome of para-social relationships in broadcasting. The use of familiar, conversational speech, the electronic illusion of immediacy – and the organising principles of seriality and regularity in TV and radio output – all combine to create the conditions in which mediated friendships might reasonably be expected to develop. Thompson was right to stress that this kind of intimacy is 'non-reciprocal'. Television or radio personalities cannot possibly know all of their audience members personally, but their performances will frequently be constructed so as to appear sociable and sincere (see Scannell 1996). Broadcasting's personae display a will to ordinariness (Langer 1981), presenting themselves as 'nothing special'.

Back in Chapter 2, I pointed out how that will is evident in the fairly informal presentation of an ITV magazine programme like *This Morning*, which is hosted by a married couple – Richard Madeley and Judy Finnigan. It is also to be heard in Anna Raeburn's afternoon phone-in show on Talk Radio, *Live and Direct*, where a mediated quasi-interaction with overhearing audiences is supplemented by two-way 'mediated interpersonal communication' between the host and her callers. In her role as an 'agony aunt', Raeburn openly declares that she has no privileged expert knowledge to impart to listeners, and she usually responds to problems on the basis of her own lay experience – while carefully attending to the 'face' (Goffman 1967; Brown and Levinson 1987) or public self-image of the person at the other end of the telephone line.

Still, as Karen Lury (1996) reminded us with her typology of performance styles on TV, there are varying degrees of formality or informality displayed by personalities in different programmes and genres, from the serious and authoritative tone of a newsreader on the BBC's *Nine O'Clock News* through to the more playful and comedic presentation of a show such as Channel 4's *The Big Breakfast*. Taking into account its position in the schedule, its content and projected audience, the producers of a television programme must arrive at what they consider to be an appropriate mode of address for consumers. However, given what Norman Fairclough (1995: 10) – a critical discourse analyst – has called the 'relaxation of the boundary between public affairs and entertainment' in broadcasting, there is now a tendency for even an established genre like TV news 'to become increasingly conversationalised'. There, in order that they might appear both 'believable' and 'personable', presenters have long sought to combine the qualities of authority and familiarity – yet the balance between these two elements is shifting as news gets gradually less formal in style. Changes of this kind are especially noticeable at the regional and transnational levels of broadcasting.

At the same time as it offers access to mediated information and entertainment, inviting identifications with its personality system, broadcasting also provides viewers and listeners with a constant 'stream' of symbolic materials from which to fashion their senses of self. Alongside those resources that are to hand in situated cultures, this flow of images and sounds is creatively appropriated by social subjects as they seek to put together personal identities and lifestyles. Television and radio programmes, their narrative structures and substantive contents, can feed into that ongoing process of identity formation in two main ways. First, they may be contributing to what social psychologist Richard Ochberg (1994) termed the 'storied nature' of contemporary selfhood. Secondly, to borrow an important idea from Anthony Giddens (1991), they supply knowledge which is then incorporated into daily actions and strategies of living – helping to facilitate the institutional reflexivity of modernity.

It is clearly the case that, in the course of our day-to-day lives, one of the means by which we attempt to sustain a coherent sense of who we are is through our 'inner speech' or narratives (Johnson 1986) – stories we routinely tell ourselves in an effort to impose some sort of order on the fragments of modern cultural experience. These stories are concerned, for instance, with structuring personal histories or planning possible futures. They are private accounts which are told inside the head, and yet they often rely on external public representations to give them shape and meaning. Certain genres of broadcast fiction such as the continuous serial and the family drama, along with human interest documentaries and interview programmes, provide suitable plots and formats for this type of internal account. So TV soap-opera viewers might compare an aspect of their own life situations with that of a fictional character. Similarly, there will be Radio 4 listeners who have thought about compiling their individual list of *Desert Island Discs*, and perhaps imagined themselves 'on air' recounting key biographical episodes from the past.

This revisable 'narrative of the self' is, in turn, part of a more general reflexivity which is essential for the functioning of modern society. Giddens (1991: 20) was careful here to distinguish between 'the reflexive monitoring of action intrinsic to all human activity' and what he preferred to call an institutional reflexivity, 'the regularised use of knowledge about the circumstances of social life as a constitutive element in its organisation'. His initial example was the role of published material on marriage, divorce and the family in providing information which can be appropriated and incorporated into decisions about how and whether to enter into specific sorts of relationship with others. He argued that anybody today who con-templates getting married or ending a long-term relationship will already be quite aware of 'what is going on' in this sphere of social action, and as Debra Grodin and Thomas Lindlof (1996: 6) have noted, modernity is 'characterised by questions that were unpre-cedented in pre-modern times ... "How do I raise my child?" or "How do I treat my spouse?"' The answers to such questions are not fixed and given. They are a matter of debate, open to revision and potentially the cause of anxiety or uncertainty. Television and radio are media through which that debate is frequently channelled. Studio discussion programmes (see Livingstone and Lunt 1994) and phone-in shows like Anna Raeburn's offer a forum for the expression of opinion and advice, while popular fictions – *Coronation Street*, *EastEnders* and *Brookside* are good examples – confront us with moral dilemmas.

If the making of self-identities is bound up in these ways with mediated communication, then senses of collective identity are dependent to a similar extent on our symbolic interactions with the media. For instance, we have touched in earlier chapters on the historical work of Paddy Scannell and David Cardiff (1991) – who charted the role of British public service broadcasting in construct-ing a knowable national culture during the inter-war years, in providing a common schedule of radio output which was available simultaneously to dispersed millions. From the privacy of their homes, listeners could tune in to the routine fare of news and entertainment, and to the BBC's live coverage of major state or sporting occasions. Despite being very much an institution of the modern age, the BBC can be seen to have played its part in 'the invention of tradition' (Hobsbawm and Ranger 1983), establishing a distinctive national calendar of events. One such media event was the monarch's annual Christmas Day message – first instituted back in the 1930s yet accepted soon afterwards as a taken-for-granted part of the festive season. On this occasion, the head of state spoke directly and intimately to the British people, addressing them both individually and collectively as national subjects. At the end of Chapter 3, though, I warned against assuming that listeners at the time would necessarily have identified with such 'interpellations' – and my qualitative research findings in Chapter 4 suggest today's audiences for multi-channel broadcasting are becoming increasingly diverse and fragmented, no longer restricted to a national audio-visual space. The electronic landscapes of television are transforming, with no prospect of a return to the kind of shared community-in-simultaneity which Scannell and Cardiff described. Having said that, there is a whole range of new collectivities to be investigated, and the mediated resources for these are being provided by computer-mediated communication as well as by broadcasting. As we shall discover in the next section, there is now a growing number of 'communities in cyberspace' (Smith and Kollock 1999).

## Telephones and Computers: Mediated Interpersonal Communication

Precisely the same set of issues – to do with arrangements of space and time, experiences of modernity, and constructions of self and community – must be central to any consideration of our social interactions via the telephone and computer. Before pursuing those themes below, it would be helpful to pause for a moment and reflect on what marks these media out as different from TV and radio. Clearly, a basic difference is the capacity which both telephones and computers have for facilitating direct one-to-one interpersonal communication at a distance, either by electronically transmitted speech or by written text. In addition to the usual person-to-person calls made routinely by phone users, 'teleconferencing' services are also available – while the computer can offer access to numerous 'multi-user domains', and topically oriented discussion groups otherwise known as 'newsgroups' (see Baym 1995). A second distinguishing feature is the heightened level of 'reciprocity' which they each allow in comparison with the quasi-interaction of broadcasting. This results in a blurring of the binary opposition between production and consumption. In communication that is mediated via telephone and computer networks it is less easy to identify 'performers' and 'audiences', at least as separate groups of people, because users of the technology are continually switching their positions as message producers or consumers.

The fact that the telephone can be used as a 'sociable medium' (Fischer 1991), as a means of maintaining friendships or for kinkeeping purposes, is evident in the advertising slogans which are employed by the telecommunications industry – 'it's good to talk', 'reach out and touch someone'. Furthermore, the fact that it falls to female callers to do much of this emotional labour has been of considerable interest to researchers like Ann Moyal (1989) in Australia and Lana Rakow (1992) in the US. In their studies of the 'feminine culture of the telephone', they each detailed the resourceful ways in which women have appropriated the medium in order to sustain social relationships across space and over time with absent friends and family. Again, technology offers entry to extended electronic communities of a sort, and the conversational interaction which it enables to take place may serve as a partial substitute for regular face-to-face contact.

However, we must not automatically assume that this mediated communication will always be a satisfactory replacement for physical co-presence with known others. Indeed, while reflecting on her interviews with women in a remote rural area, Rakow (1992) suggested that their use of the telephone might equally be seen as a sign of 'isolation ... boredom or fear'. She was careful to avoid the trap of thinking that mediated experiences can ever simply transcend the problems of 'real life' in a situated locality, an important point to which I return shortly in my discussion of computer cultures. The reliance of her interviewees on telephone communication was largely down to the restricted control which they exerted over their own physical location. For instance, several found themselves isolated in the country as a result of having moved there with men. So even if phone networks could 'make all points equidistant ... the point from which these women are starting is not necessarily of their own choosing' (Rakow 1992: 62). Here, then, is a valuable reminder of the material limitations which help to shape symbolic exchanges in modern society. Telephone use, in this particular example, may well constitute a creative set of gendered cultural practices – but ultimately they are acted out within determinate social constraints.

Thus far, I have focused our attention on mediated interactions and quasi-interactions where the participants are seeking to reproduce a routine experience of familiarity – callers speaking with friends and relatives by phone, or television viewers identifying with screen personalities. Yet on certain occasions, it could be the case that more fleeting and anonymous encounters are being sought. Gary Gumpert (1990) has presented a revealing account of such communication in his analysis of 'remote sex' via the telephone and personal computer. He was concerned with the dynamics and consequences of this erotic discourse between strangers, in which callers and 'keyboarders' engage in a live spoken or written event. Subscribing to services with names like *Fantasy Phone Inc.*, *The Hot Line* and *Eroticomm*, users are spatially separated but they participate in temporally simultaneous electronic conferences – involving two people or sometimes larger groups. One of the features of that jointly constructed dialogue is the ability it gives interlocutors to indulge in fantasy narratives and to develop fictional personae for themselves which are quite different from those they inhabit in their ordinary, everyday lives.

Aside from these forms of specifically pornographic communication, there are also numerous other 'text-based virtual realities' now available to us on the Internet, interactive electronic environments in which a participant's own presentation of self is heavily dependent on the description of character and appearance that is offered to others who are known only on the same terms. As a number of recent commentators have argued, such role-playing games – which are enacted collaboratively within the computer network's multi-user domains, or MUDs – allow self-identity to be experimented with on-line in new and interesting ways. Those commentators include Elizabeth Reid (1995), Heather Bromberg (1996) and Caroline Bassett (1997) – all of whom discussed practices of 'identity play' on MUDs where the participants have mediated encounters with each other as they pass through 'rooms' in virtual architecture. Here, users will usually construct an alias or a series of aliases for themselves, sometimes 'morphing' between different characters and appearances. Inventive as the practices are, they inevitably raise questions about the sincerity and integrity of self-presentation. Participants cannot be sure precisely who they are in dialogue with, or to what extent screen identities correspond with those performed in life away from the computer. Perhaps the most astute social theorist currently working on this topic is Sherry Turkle (1996). Carrying out her ethnographic field research in both actual places and simulated locations, she has looked at the putting together of personal identities in between what MUD inhabitants call RL – real life – and the expanding frontiers of cyberspace.

One fundamental starting point here is the idea that contemporary subjectivities are fragmented and multiple. As discussed above in the preceding section of my chapter, we will usually try to construct a coherent sense of selfhood through our inner speech and storytelling – but it is important for us to ask what happens when these narratives appear on a computer screen, and when the stories cast their subjects in roles which are not those played in day-to-day life off-line. For example, a normally shy graduate student living in modest university accommodation builds an elegant apartment for himself on the MUD, and through an alias becomes romantically involved with a fellow player who logs on from another continent. His fantasy character develops an on-line friendship with hers, which then leads to an 'engagement' and finally to a simulated 'wedding ceremony', a virtual event that is 'witnessed' and cele-brated by other computer users. In cyberspace, he is able to interact with a confidence which is lacking in RL, and tells Turkle (1996: 193) how he would like 'to feel that his MUD life is part of his real life'. Yet when it comes to his own co-present interactions in local settings, this young man finds it difficult to draw on any of the confidence he has gained in communication with his absent lover on the global Net. In the end, situated and mediated experience remain deeply divided and his self-identity is split or 'distributed' across different sites.

If MUDs are primarily sites for game playing, albeit serious play for some computer users, then other areas on the Net are devoted to public debate and to a sharing of knowledge on specialist topics – leading a technological optimist like William Mitchell (1995) to enthuse over the formation of 'electronic agoras' for the so-called 'soft cities' of the next millennium. He stated that the Internet will have 'as crucial a role in twenty-first century urbanity as the centrally located, spatially bounded, architecturally celebrated agora did ... according to Aristotle's *Politics* ... in the life of the Greek polis' (Mitchell 1995: 8). His utopian vision is one in which on-line communities of various sorts might enable us, despite our largely privatised existence, to combat an erosion of civil society – as we gather together in virtual locations that substitute for collective meeting places where opinions and ideas are exchanged.

A rather more cautious or pessimistic view has been offered by Kevin Robins (1996), who remained suspicious of those enthusiastic terms in which certain writers had described virtual communities. Although their visions may appear to be futuristic, he detected a fundamentally nostalgic imagination at work there, a kind of 'techno-communitarianism' that advocates 'extending the security of small-town "gemeinschaft" to the transnational scale of the global village' (Robins 1996: 21). Instead of seeking simulated utopian alternatives to our presently existing culture, Robins has invited us to look at cyberspace firmly in the context of 'the world we live in', by which he meant a material world of social inequalities and power relations. Similarly, when considering the implications of computer-mediated communication for modern public life, Jim McGuigan (1996) reminded his readers of a wide gap between the 'information-haves' and the 'information-have-nots' – pointing out that most of this earth's population still has no easy access to old IT such as the telephone, let alone new computer technologies.

## Encounters Between Co-Present Participants

Further sobering thoughts have been voiced by Deirdre Boden and Harvey Molotch (1994). It was their bold assertion that – in all the excitement generated by recent developments in media technology – the enduring significance of routine, co-present interaction has actually been underappreciated. They produced a wealth of empirical evidence which suggests that, even in our technologically advanced modern society where human relationships might be extended across space and time, the compulsion of proximity is alive and well. For instance, while communicating with absent friends and family by telephone and electronic mail, it is not unusual for us to say things like 'I miss you' or 'let's meet up soon' – and when we do meet up, to use phrases such as 'it's great to see you again'. There will obviously be times when mediated interactions are preferred for various reasons over situated encounters. However, the pertinent point here is that electronic communication has not totally removed the desire to be both physically and emotionally close to others. Far from it, because we continue to live in what Giddens (1990: 143) named a 'peopled world ... not merely one of anonymous, blank faces'. Modernity, then, is characterised by certain sorts of proximate intimacy – as well as by mediated intimacy at a distance or by the polite, impersonal rituals of civil inattention (Goffman 1963) between strangers in many urban settings today.

The strength of that case for the continued study of situated interactions need not lead social theorists and researchers away from the media, though. I want to argue that an analysis of the mediated interaction order must also account for the complex ways in which communication and information technologies are 'knotted into' everyday encounters between co-present participants. Those relationships which people form in places like households, neighbourhoods, work and leisure contexts are frequently negotiated around electronic media – in the course of using television, radio, telephones or computers. So in the little dramas of day-to-day living, these technological objects and their symbolic contents may serve as part of what Goffman (1969) once called the stage 'props' and 'scenery' for interpersonal behaviour.

In his investigation of the 'social uses' of broadcasting in domestic situations, James Lull (1990) talked about TV being employed in precisely this fashion – as an affiliation resource with which audience members can engineer shared moments of intimacy, physical contact and family solidarity. One of his examples was a household where, during a period of participant observation, the husband and wife were seen to touch on two specific occasions. On the first of these, he noted that the medium for their playful embrace was the daughter, who returned from school with a humorous story to tell – but on the second occasion, it was the medium of television which provided them with an opportunity for closeness. The husband was tired and 'fell asleep when he watched television at night', while the wife 'who had been sitting on the floor in the same room ... leaned back until her head rested against his bare feet and smiled' (Lull 1990: 38). Although this particular instance of proximity is profoundly mundane, such ordinary events are the very stuff of social interaction in families.

Of course, households might just as easily be sites of discord and avoidance as havens of harmony and domestic solidarity (see Bausinger 1984). There is a 'politics of the living room', and the media are often located at the centre of interpersonal struggles in consumption contexts. Remember how David Morley (1986) remarked upon the position of the remote control device in TV viewing arrangements, finding this gadget to be typically in the father's possession, on the 'arm of Daddy's chair'. Disputes over which programme or channel to watch are frequently resolved in ways that reflect a patriarchal structure of authority in the home. Turning our attention to a different domestic technology, we could point to gendered and generational frictions in family life over access to the telephone, and over the size of the quarterly phone bill. Most people will have experienced these tensions at some time – for example, as teenagers fighting for the right to talk privately with friends and thereby mark out independent identities, or as parents worried about the accumulated expense of those calls. It is therefore necessary for us to see the technology not simply as a means of interacting with absent others, but as a 'fixed prop' for co-present encounters and for situated practices of self-presentation.

Beyond the front door, in the neighbourhood setting, there are also occasions when media technologies can serve as props for the performance of identity – or else for struggles over the meaning of local community. The arrival of satellite dish aerials in the UK during the late 1980s and early 1990s gave rise to what Charlotte Brunsdon (1991) referred to as a 'controversy about siting', a kind of taste war fought out between dish-erectors and 'anti-dishers'. For members of the former group, the object was a public sign of their investment in the new. Meanwhile, for the latter group – especially those living in 'respectable' areas of older housing – it posed a threat to the financial and heritage values of their residential properties. As I demonstrated in Chapter 4, discourses of innovation and conservation confront each other head on in these circumstances – resulting in a range of emotional dispositions being displayed towards the dish on the outside wall of the house, from senses of pride or embarrassment through to feelings of distaste and disgust.

Reception analysts in media and cultural studies have begun to document the circulation of TV narratives in public workplaces and leisure interactions, too. Dorothy Hobson (1989) has investigated routine talk about soap opera among female office workers in Birmingham, noting that the consumption of this popular entertainment does not come to an end in the privacy of the home. Instead, continuous serials provide some of the material which is used to generate day-to-day gossip with workmates. Hobson (1989: 150) saw how such talk is 'fitted in around their working time or in lunch breaks', and she heard it taking 'the form of storytelling, commenting on the stories ... moving from the drama to discussing the incidents which are happening in the "real world"'. Charting a similar process in a different context, in this case the peer-group interactions of British Asian youths in London, Marie Gillespie (1993: 27) argued that these 'young people's everyday verbal discourse is informed in significant ways by their soap viewing not simply in its content but also ... in its form'. Discussion of *Neighbours* – a globally distributed Australian fiction – was inextricably linked with utterances about other, more local matters. At first, the two appeared almost indistinguishable to her, as the focus of gossip shifted unselfconsciously between mediated culture and immediate social circumstances. Among the young Pakistani Scots from Edinburgh featured in Chapter 7, the same television fiction was a common point of reference in verbal interaction.

Just as Hobson challenged the idea that investigations of TV viewing can be confined to the domestic situations in which it usually takes place, so Leslie Haddon (1992) contended that 'home computing' must not be seen as a solely home-based cultural activity. Reflecting back on his study of teenage boys and microcomputers, conducted in the 1980s, he encouraged us to look at school and leisure settings as important locales for the production of 'computer talk' – a specific type of competitive banter in which the boys would evaluate hardware and software, and compare notes on their game-playing abilities. The consumption of those goods in the household was shaped in part by outside interactions with peers. In turn, their private use of technology became a resource for public leisure in the context of the schoolyard or computer club.

None of this points towards a disappearance of co-present communication. Rather, it illustrates the changing interaction mix of daily life in the modern world (Thompson 1995), in which media use and proximate interpersonal exchanges are either mutually dependent or simultaneously enacted. A further example of this blurred category of social behaviour is the current emergence of coffee houses in the high street with names like *The CyberCafé* and *Cyberia*. In these places, there is an intriguing blend of old and new cultural activities. Customers pay for food and drink, chatting to staff and to other customers as they might do in any café or bar setting – but in addition, they buy access to a computer screen and keyboard, 'surfing' the Net to contact absent interlocutors. It could be said that sociability is being sustained on two separate fronts at once here – as conversations are held both with those who are nearby and with those who are, at least in physical terms, far away.

## Some Conceptual and Practical Implications

Finally, let us look at some conceptual and practical implications of delimiting our object of inquiry in the manner proposed by my concluding chapter. I will consider three such implications. First of all, we require an expanded and more inclusive definition of electronic media than that which has traditionally been employed in media analysis. There is still a strong tendency, even today, to equate media studies rather too narrowly with an investigation of mass communication – and even if the recent interest in reception has enabled us to see how television and radio use are intricately bound up with situated interactions in day-to-day life, we do need to pay much greater attention to mediated interpersonal communication conducted via the telephone and computer. Of course, as is clearly acknowledged in my preceding commentary, these different forms of mediated interaction and quasi-interaction have their own distinctive features – yet I am proposing that there is much to be gained by studying them side by side in the broader context of debates about communication and modernity. In any event, arguments for a 'convergence' of academic work around the notion of a mediated interaction order are soon likely to be overtaken by technological convergence in the media industries. Manufacturers themselves are seeking to develop a new generation of information and entertainment services which can increasingly bridge the gap between broadcasting, telecommunications and computing.

Secondly, it is also necessary for us to adopt a modified vocabulary of critical terms for the purposes of media inquiry. So alongside those key concepts which are found in contemporary media and cultural studies – 'ideology', 'power', 'discourse' and so forth – I am suggesting that we recover an alternative series of terms like 'presentation of self', 'para-social interaction' and 'sociability'. These come out of a different strand of modern social theory which has been concerned directly with the performative or experiential dimensions of culture, aspects of symbolic exchange which in my view deserve our careful scrutiny. This is certainly not to deny the ideological or political dimensions of electronically mediated communication, but to propose that they are best approached via basic issues of human interaction and lived experience. Neither is this merely an academic game of words, because concepts which are chosen to describe and interpret an object of study are absolutely crucial in shaping the perspective taken by social researchers.

Thirdly, I would argue that we must now develop more sophisticated research strategies with which to investigate the complex 'interaction mixes of daily life' in modern society. Admittedly, this is easier said than done. It is difficult for us to chart a combination of often simultaneous activities involving situated, mediated interpersonal and mediated quasi-interaction – especially when those activities interweave 'presence' and 'absence', and when some of them are stretched across space and time. There is the thorny question of where our mapping of these kinds of hybrid communication should begin. My pragmatic answer is to say that, despite the highly mobile and dispersed character of communication in contemporary culture, it has to start with the everyday practices of particular social subjects in specific locales. Recognising the permeability of place, we could then go on to explore the distant and virtual sites to which people travel imaginatively in their routine existence, utilising electronic media ourselves in the course of the research. The methods of participant or non-participant observation and conversational interviewing, and the analysis of media forms and solicited documentary materials, may continue to provide us with valuable data for constructing detailed ethnographic portraits of interaction patterns. It follows that one practical way of examining modernity's mixed interactions is by grounding them in ongoing biographical projects. At several points in my chapter, I have referred to the idea that senses of self-identity and imagined community are put together as part of a reflexive project, as subjects draw selectively on the available symbolic resources. By accessing their narratives of individual and collective identity, it might be possible to discover precisely how they are attempting to combine the range of situated and mediated communication in an 'orderly' and organised fashion.

# References

Adam, Barbara (1995), *Timewatch: The Social Analysis of Time*, Cambridge: Polity Press.

Afshar, Haleh (1989), 'Gender Roles and the "Moral Economy of Kin" Among Pakistani Women in West Yorkshire', *New Community*, Vol. 15, No. 2, pp. 211–25.

Afshar, Haleh (1994), 'Muslim Women in West Yorkshire: Growing Up with Real and Imaginary Values Amidst Conflicting Views of Self and Society', in Haleh Afshar and Mary Maynard (eds), *The Dynamics of 'Race' and Gender: Some Feminist Interventions*, London: Taylor and Francis, pp. 127–47.

Alexander, Claire (1996), *The Art of Being Black: The Creation of Black British Youth Identities*, Oxford: Oxford University Press.

Allan, Graham (1989a), 'Insiders and Outsiders: Boundaries Around the Home', in Graham Allan and Graham Crow (eds), *Home and Family: Creating the Domestic Sphere*, Basingstoke: Macmillan, pp. 141–58.

Allan, Graham (1989b), *Friendship: Developing a Sociological Perspective*, Hemel Hempstead: Harvester Wheatsheaf.

Althusser, Louis (1984), *Essays on Ideology*, London: Verso.

Anderson, Benedict (1983), *Imagined Communities: Reflections on the Origin and Spread of Nationalism*, London: Verso.

Ang, Ien (1985), *Watching 'Dallas': Soap Opera and the Melodramatic Imagination*, London: Methuen.

Ang, Ien (1991), *Desperately Seeking the Audience*, London: Routledge.

Ang, Ien (1992), 'Living Room Wars: New Technologies, Audience Measurement and the Tactics of Television Consumption', in Roger Silverstone and Eric Hirsch (eds), *Consuming Technologies: Media and Information in Domestic Spaces*, London: Routledge, pp. 131–45.

Anthias, Floya (1999), 'Theorising Identity, Difference and Social Divisions', in Martin O'Brien, Sue Penna and Colin Hay (eds), *Theorising Modernity: Reflexivity, Environment and Identity in Giddens' Social Theory*, Harlow: Longman, pp. 156–78.

Bachelard, Gaston (1969), *The Poetics of Space*, Boston: Beacon Press.

Back, Les (1996), *New Ethnicities and Urban Culture: Racisms and Multiculture in Young Lives*, London: UCL Press.

Ballard, Roger (1982), 'South Asian Families', in Robert Rapoport, Michael

Fogarty and Rhona Rapoport (eds), *Families in Britain*, London: Routledge and Kegan Paul, pp. 179–204.

Barrett, Michèle and Mary McIntosh (1982), *The Anti-Social Family*, London: Verso.

Bassett, Caroline (1997), 'Virtually Gendered: Life in an On-Line World', in Ken Gelder and Sarah Thornton (eds), *The Subcultures Reader*, London: Routledge, pp. 537–50.

Baudrillard, Jean (1988), *Selected Writings*, Cambridge: Polity Press.

Bausinger, Hermann (1984), 'Media, Technology and Daily Life', *Media, Culture and Society*, Vol. 6, No. 4, pp. 343–51.

Baym, Nancy (1995), 'From Practice to Culture on Usenet', in Susan Star (ed.), *The Cultures of Computing*, Oxford: Blackwell/Sociological Review, pp. 29–52.

Beck, Ulrich (1992), *Risk Society: Towards a New Modernity*, London: Sage.

Bell, Allan and Peter Garrett (eds) (1998), *Approaches to Media Discourse*, Oxford: Blackwell.

Berman, Marshall (1983), *All That is Solid Melts into Air: The Experience of Modernity*, London: Verso.

Bhabha, Homi (ed.) (1990), *Nation and Narration*, London: Routledge.

Billig, Michael (1992), *Talking of the Royal Family*, London: Routledge.

Boden, Deirdre and Harvey Molotch (1994), 'The Compulsion of Proximity', in Roger Friedland and Deirdre Boden (eds), *NowHere: Space, Time and Modernity*, Berkeley: University of California Press, pp. 257–86.

Bourdieu, Pierre (1984), *Distinction: A Social Critique of the Judgement of Taste*, London: Routledge and Kegan Paul.

Brah, Avtar (1996), *Cartographies of Diaspora: Contesting Identities*, London: Routledge.

Bromberg, Heather (1996), 'Are MUDs Communities? Identity, Belonging and Consciousness in Virtual Worlds', in Rob Shields (ed.), *Cultures of Internet: Virtual Spaces, Real Histories, Living Bodies*, London: Sage, pp. 143–52.

Brooker-Gross, Susan (1985), 'The Changing Concept of Place in the News', in Jacquelin Burgess and John Gold (eds), *Geography, the Media and Popular Culture*, London: Croom Helm, pp. 63–85.

Brown, Aggrey (1998), 'Up Close from a Distance: Media and the Culture of Cricket', in Roger Dickinson, Ramaswami Harindranath and Olga Linné (eds), *Approaches to Audiences: A Reader*, London: Arnold, pp. 14–24.

Brown, Penelope and Stephen Levinson (1987), *Politeness: Some Universals in Language Usage*, Cambridge: Cambridge University Press.

Brunn, Stanley and Thomas Leinbach (eds) (1991), *Collapsing Space and Time: Geographic Aspects of Communication and Information*, London: HarperCollins.

Brunsdon, Charlotte (1981), '"Crossroads": Notes on Soap Opera', *Screen*, Vol. 22, No. 4, pp. 32–7.

Brunsdon, Charlotte (1989), 'Text and Audience', in Ellen Seiter, Hans Borchers, Gabriele Kreutzner and Eva-Maria Warth (eds), *Remote Control: Television, Audiences and Cultural Power*, London: Routledge, pp. 116–29.

Brunsdon, Charlotte (1991), 'Satellite Dishes and the Landscapes of Taste', *New Formations*, No. 15, pp. 23–42.

Brunsdon, Charlotte and David Morley (1978), *Everyday Television: 'Nationwide'*, London: British Film Institute.

Burgess, Jacquelin and John Gold (eds) (1985), *Geography, the Media and Popular Culture*, London: Croom Helm.

Cardiff, David and Paddy Scannell (1987), 'Broadcasting and National Unity', in James Curran, Anthony Smith and Pauline Wingate (eds), *Impacts and Influences: Essays on Media Power in the Twentieth Century*, London: Methuen, pp. 157–73.

Carey, James (1989), *Communication as Culture: Essays on Media and Society*, Boston: Unwin Hyman.

Chaney, David (1987), 'Audience Research and the BBC in the 1930s: A Mass Medium Comes into Being', in James Curran, Anthony Smith and Pauline Wingate (eds), *Impacts and Influences: Essays on Media Power in the Twentieth Century*, London: Methuen, pp. 259–77.

Chaney, David (1993), *Fictions of Collective Life: Public Drama in Late Modern Culture*, London: Routledge.

Charles, Nickie and Marion Kerr (1988), *Women, Food and Families*, Manchester: Manchester University Press.

Clifford, James (1986), 'Introduction: Partial Truths', in James Clifford and George Marcus (eds), *Writing Culture: The Poetics and Politics of Ethnography*, Berkeley: University of California Press, pp. 1–26.

Clifford, James (1992), 'Travelling Cultures', in Lawrence Grossberg, Cary Nelson and Paula Treichler (eds), *Cultural Studies*, New York: Routledge, pp. 96–116.

Clifford, James (1997), *Routes: Travel and Translation in the Late Twentieth Century*, Cambridge, MA: Harvard University Press.

Cockburn, Cynthia (1985), *Machinery of Dominance: Women, Men and Technical Know-How*, London: Pluto.

Collins, Richard (1990a), *Television: Policy and Culture*, London: Unwin Hyman.

Collins, Richard (1990b), *Satellite Television in Western Europe*, London: John Libbey.

Corner, John (ed.) (1991), *Popular Television in Britain: Studies in Cultural History*, London: British Film Institute.

Corner, John (1995), *Television Form and Public Address*, London: Edward Arnold.

Corner, John, Sylvia Harvey and Karen Lury (1994), 'Culture, Quality and Choice: The Re-Regulation of TV 1989–91', in Stuart Hood (ed.), *Behind the Screens: The Structure of British Television in the 1990s*, London: Lawrence and Wishart, pp. 1–19.

Corner, John, Kay Richardson and Natalie Fenton (1990a), 'Textualising Risk: TV Discourse and the Issue of Nuclear Energy', *Media, Culture and Society*, Vol. 12, No. 1, pp. 105–24.

Corner, John, Kay Richardson and Natalie Fenton (1990b), *Nuclear Reactions: Form and Response in 'Public Issue' Television*, London: John Libbey.

Dayan, Daniel and Elihu Katz (1992), *Media Events: The Live Broadcasting of History*, Cambridge, MA: Harvard University Press.

Deem, Rosemary (1986), *All Work and No Play? The Sociology of Women and Leisure*, Milton Keynes: Open University Press.

Delphy, Christine (1984), *Close to Home: A Materialist Analysis of Women's Oppression*, London: Hutchinson.

Donzelot, Jacques (1980), *The Policing of Families*, London: Hutchinson.

du Gay, Paul, Stuart Hall, Linda Janes, Hugh Mackay and Keith Negus (1997), *Doing Cultural Studies: The Story of the Sony Walkman*, London: Sage/Open University.

Ellis, John (1982), *Visible Fictions: Cinema, Television, Video*, London: Routledge and Kegan Paul.

Fairclough, Norman (1992), *Discourse and Social Change*, Cambridge: Polity Press.

Fairclough, Norman (1994), 'Conversationalisation of Public Discourse and the Authority of the Consumer', in Russell Keat, Nigel Whiteley and Nicholas Abercrombie (eds), *The Authority of the Consumer*, London: Routledge, pp. 253–68.

Fairclough, Norman (1995), *Media Discourse*, London: Edward Arnold.

Ferguson, Marjorie (1990), 'Electronic Media and the Redefining of Time and Space', in Marjorie Ferguson (ed.), *Public Communication – The New Imperatives: Future Directions for Media Research*, London: Sage, pp. 152–72.

Fischer, Claude (1991), '"Touch Someone": The Telephone Industry Discovers Sociability', in Marcel Lafollette and Jeffrey Stine (eds), *Technology and Choice: Readings from Technology and Culture*, Chicago: University of Chicago Press, pp. 87–116.

Formations Collective (ed.) (1984), *Formations of Nation and People*, London: Routledge and Kegan Paul.

Foucault, Michel (1977), *Discipline and Punish: The Birth of the Prison*, London: Allen Lane.

Foucault, Michel (1980), *Power/Knowledge: Selected Interviews and Other Writings 1972–1977*, Brighton: Harvester.

Frith, Simon (1983), 'The Pleasures of the Hearth: The Making of BBC Light Entertainment', in Formations Collective (ed.), *Formations of Pleasure*, London: Routledge and Kegan Paul, pp. 101–23.

Frith, Simon (1996), 'Music and Identity', in Stuart Hall and Paul du Gay (eds), *Questions of Cultural Identity*, London: Sage, pp. 108–27.

Gauntlett, David and Annette Hill (1999), *TV Living: Television, Culture and Everyday Life*, London: Routledge.

Geertz, Clifford (1973), *The Interpretation of Cultures: Selected Essays*, New York: Basic Books.

Geertz, Clifford (1983), *Local Knowledge: Further Essays in Interpretive Anthropology*, London: Fontana.

Geraghty, Christine (1981), 'The Continuous Serial: A Definition', in Richard Dyer, Christine Geraghty, Marion Jordan, Terry Lovell, Richard Paterson and John Stewart (eds), *Coronation Street*, London: British Film Institute, pp. 9–26.

Geraghty, Christine (1991), *Women and Soap Opera: A Study of Prime-Time Soaps*, Cambridge: Polity Press.

Giddens, Anthony (1981), *A Contemporary Critique of Historical Materialism*, Basingstoke: Macmillan.

Giddens, Anthony (1984), *The Constitution of Society: Outline of the Theory of Structuration*, Cambridge: Polity Press.

Giddens, Anthony (1990), *The Consequences of Modernity*, Cambridge: Polity Press.

Giddens, Anthony (1991), *Modernity and Self-Identity: Self and Society in the Late Modern Age*, Cambridge: Polity Press.

Giddens, Anthony and Christopher Pierson (1998), *Conversations with Anthony Giddens: Making Sense of Modernity*, Cambridge: Polity Press.

Gillespie, Marie (1989), 'Technology and Tradition: Audio-Visual Culture Among South Asian Families in West London', *Cultural Studies*, Vol. 3, No. 2, pp. 226–39.

Gillespie, Marie (1993), 'Soap Viewing, Gossip and Rumour Amongst Punjabi Youth in Southall', in Phillip Drummond, Richard Paterson and Janet Willis (eds), *National Identity and Europe: The Television Revolution*, London: British Film Institute, pp. 25–42.

Gillespie, Marie (1995), *Television, Ethnicity and Cultural Change*, London: Routledge.

Gilroy, Paul (1993), *The Black Atlantic: Modernity and Double Consciousness*, London: Verso.

Goffman, Erving (1963), *Behavior in Public Places: Notes on the Social Organisation of Gatherings*, New York: Free Press.

Goffman, Erving (1967), *Interaction Ritual: Essays on Face-to-Face Behavior*, New York: Pantheon.

Goffman, Erving (1969), *The Presentation of Self in Everyday Life*, London: Allen Lane.

Goffman, Erving (1981), *Forms of Talk*, Oxford: Blackwell.

Goffman, Erving (1983), 'The Interaction Order', *American Sociological Review*, Vol. 48, No. 1, pp. 1–17.

Gray, Ann (1987), 'Behind Closed Doors: Video Recorders in the Home', in Helen Baehr and Gillian Dyer (eds), *Boxed In: Women and Television*, London: Pandora, pp. 38–54.

Gray, Ann (1992), *Video Playtime: The Gendering of a Leisure Technology*, London: Routledge.

Gregory, Derek and John Urry (eds) (1985), *Social Relations and Spatial Structures*, Basingstoke: Macmillan.

Grodin, Debra and Thomas Lindlof (1996), 'The Self and Mediated Communication', in Debra Grodin and Thomas Lindlof (eds), *Constructing the Self in a Mediated World*, Thousand Oaks: Sage, pp. 3–12.

Gumpert, Gary (1990), 'Remote Sex in the Information Age', in Gary Gumpert and Sandra Fish (eds), *Talking to Strangers: Mediated Therapeutic Communication*, Norwood: Ablex, pp. 143–53.

Gumpert, Gary and Robert Cathcart (eds) (1982), *Inter/Media: Interpersonal Communication in a Media World*, 2nd edn, New York: Oxford University Press.

Haddon, Leslie (1988), 'The Home Computer: The Making of a Consumer Electronic', *Science as Culture*, No. 2, pp. 7–51.

Haddon, Leslie (1992), 'Explaining ICT Consumption: The Case of the Home Computer', in Roger Silverstone and Eric Hirsch (eds), *Consuming Technologies: Media and Information in Domestic Spaces*, London: Routledge, pp. 82–96.

Hall, Stuart (1973), 'Encoding and Decoding in the Television Discourse', Stencilled Paper, Centre for Contemporary Cultural Studies, University of Birmingham.

Hall, Stuart (1986a), 'On Postmodernism and Articulation', *Journal of Communication Inquiry*, Vol. 10, No. 2, pp. 45–60.

Hall, Stuart (1986b), 'Cultural Studies: Two Paradigms', in Richard Collins, James Curran, Nicholas Garnham, Paddy Scannell, Philip Schlesinger and Colin Sparks (eds), *Media, Culture and Society: A Critical Reader*, London: Sage, pp. 33–48.

Hall, Stuart (1992), 'The Question of Cultural Identity', in Stuart Hall, David Held and Tony McGrew (eds), *Modernity and Its Futures*, Cambridge: Polity Press/Open University, pp. 273–316.

Hall, Stuart (1997), 'The Centrality of Culture: Notes on the Cultural Revolutions of Our Time', in Kenneth Thompson (ed.), *Media and Cultural Regulation*, London: Sage/Open University, pp. 207–38.

Hannerz, Ulf (1996), *Transnational Connections: Culture, People, Places*, London: Routledge.

Harvey, David (1989), *The Condition of Postmodernity: An Enquiry into the Origins of Cultural Change*, Oxford: Blackwell.

Hebdige, Dick (1979), *Subculture: The Meaning of Style*, London: Methuen.

Hebdige, Dick (1982), 'Towards a Cartography of Taste 1935–1962', in Bernard Waites, Tony Bennett and Graham Martin (eds), *Popular Culture: Past and Present*, London: Croom Helm/Open University, pp. 194–218.

Hebdige, Dick (1988), *Hiding in the Light: On Images and Things*, London: Routledge.

Hirsch, Eric (1992), 'The Long Term and the Short Term of Domestic Consumption: An Ethnographic Case Study', in Roger Silverstone and Eric Hirsch (eds), *Consuming Technologies: Media and Information in Domestic Spaces*, London: Routledge, pp. 208–26.

Hobsbawm, Eric and Terence Ranger (eds) (1983), *The Invention of Tradition*, Cambridge: Cambridge University Press.

Hobson, Dorothy (1980), 'Housewives and the Mass Media', in Stuart Hall, Dorothy Hobson, Andrew Lowe and Paul Willis (eds), *Culture, Media, Language: Working Papers in Cultural Studies, 1972–79*, London: Hutchinson, pp. 105–14.

Hobson, Dorothy (1982), *'Crossroads': The Drama of a Soap Opera*, London: Methuen.

Hobson, Dorothy (1989), 'Soap Operas at Work', in Ellen Seiter, Hans Borchers, Gabriele Kreutzner and Eva-Maria Warth (eds), *Remote Control: Television, Audiences and Cultural Power*, London: Routledge, pp. 150–67.

Hochschild, Arlie Russell (1983), *The Managed Heart: Commercialisation of Human Feeling*, Berkeley: University of California Press.

Horton, Donald and Richard Wohl (1956), 'Mass Communication and Para-Social Interaction: Observations on Intimacy at a Distance', *Psychiatry*, Vol. 19, No. 3, pp. 215–29.

Innis, Harold (1951), *The Bias of Communication*, Toronto: University of Toronto Press.

Jackson, Peter (1989), *Maps of Meaning: An Introduction to Cultural Geography*, London: Unwin Hyman.

Jackson, Stevi and Shaun Moores (eds) (1995), *The Politics of Domestic Consumption: Critical Readings*, Hemel Hempstead: Prentice Hall/Harvester Wheatsheaf.

Jennings, Hilda and Winnifred Gill (1939), *Broadcasting in Everyday Life: A Survey of the Social Effects of the Coming of Broadcasting*, London: BBC.

Jensen, Klaus Bruhn (1995), *The Social Semiotics of Mass Communication*, London: Sage.

Johnson, Lesley (1981), 'Radio and Everyday Life: The Early Years of Broadcasting in Australia, 1922–1945', *Media, Culture and Society*, Vol. 3, No. 2, pp. 167–78.

Johnson, Lesley (1993), *The Modern Girl: Girlhood and Growing Up*, Buckingham: Open University Press.

Johnson, Richard (1986), 'The Story So Far: And Further Transformations?', in David Punter (ed.), *Introduction to Contemporary Cultural Studies*, Harlow: Longman, pp. 277–313.

Kopytoff, Igor (1986), 'The Cultural Biography of Things: Commoditisation as Process', in Arjun Appadurai (ed.), *The Social Life of Things: Commodities in Cultural Perspective*, Cambridge: Cambridge University Press, pp. 64–91.

Langer, John (1981), 'Television's Personality System', *Media, Culture and Society*, Vol. 3, No. 4, pp. 351–65.

Leal, Ondina Fachel (1990), 'Popular Taste and Erudite Repertoire: The Place and Space of Television in Brazil', *Cultural Studies*, Vol. 4, No. 1, pp. 19–29.

Levy, Mark (1982), 'Watching TV News as Para-Social Interaction', in Gary Gumpert and Robert Cathcart (eds), *Inter/Media: Interpersonal Communication in a Media World*, 2nd edn, New York: Oxford University Press, pp. 177–87.

Leyshon, Andrew (1995), 'Annihilating Space? The Speed-Up of Communications', in John Allen and Chris Hamnett (eds), *A Shrinking World? Global Unevenness and Inequality*, Oxford: Oxford University Press/Open University, pp. 11–46.

Livingstone, Sonia and Peter Lunt (1994), *Talk on Television: Audience Participation and Public Debate*, London: Routledge.

Lull, James (1990), *Inside Family Viewing: Ethnographic Research on Television's Audiences*, London: Routledge.

Lury, Karen (1996), 'Television Performance: Being, Acting and "Corpsing"', *New Formations*, No. 27, pp. 114–27.

Mackay, Hugh and Gareth Gillespie (1992), 'Extending the Social Shaping of Technology Approach: Ideology and Appropriation', *Social Studies of Science*, Vol. 22, No. 4, pp. 685–716.

MacKenzie, Donald and Judy Wajcman (eds) (1985), *The Social Shaping of Technology: How the Refrigerator Got Its Hum*, Milton Keynes: Open University Press.

Marcus, George (1992), 'Past, Present and Emergent Identities: Requirements for Ethnographies of Late Twentieth-Century Modernity Worldwide', in Scott Lash and Jonathan Friedman (eds), *Modernity and Identity*, Oxford: Blackwell, pp. 309–30.

Massey, Doreen (1992), 'A Place Called Home?', *New Formations*, No. 17, pp. 3–15.

McGuigan, Jim (1996), *Culture and the Public Sphere*, London: Routledge.

McLuhan, Marshall (1964), *Understanding Media: The Extensions of Man*, London: Routledge and Kegan Paul.

Meyrowitz, Joshua (1985), *No Sense of Place: The Impact of Electronic Media on Social Behavior*, New York: Oxford University Press.

Meyrowitz, Joshua (1994), 'Medium Theory', in David Crowley and David Mitchell (eds), *Communication Theory Today*, Cambridge: Polity Press, pp. 50–77.

Mitchell, William (1995), *City of Bits: Space, Place and the Infobahn*, Cambridge, MA: MIT Press.

Moores, Shaun (1990), 'Texts, Readers and Contexts of Reading: Developments in the Study of Media Audiences', *Media, Culture and Society*, Vol. 12, No. 1, pp. 9–29.

Moores, Shaun (1993), *Interpreting Audiences: The Ethnography of Media Consumption*, London: Sage.

Moores, Shaun (in press), 'Qualitative Research Methods', in Dan Fleming (ed.), *Formations: 21st Century Media Studies*, Manchester: Manchester University Press.

Morley, David (1980), *The 'Nationwide' Audience: Structure and Decoding*, London: British Film Institute.

Morley, David (1981), 'The "Nationwide" Audience: A Critical Postscript', *Screen Education*, No. 39, pp. 3–14.

Morley, David (1986), *Family Television: Cultural Power and Domestic Leisure*, London: Comedia.

Morley, David (1988), 'Domestic Relations: The Framework of Family Viewing in Great Britain', in James Lull (ed.), *World Families Watch Television*, Newbury Park: Sage, pp. 22–48.

Morley, David (1990), 'Behind the Ratings', in Janet Willis and Tana Wollen (eds), *The Neglected Audience*, London: British Film Institute, pp. 5–14.

Morley, David (1992), *Television, Audiences and Cultural Studies*, London: Routledge.

Morley, David and Kevin Robins (1995), *Spaces of Identity: Global Media, Electronic Landscapes and Cultural Boundaries*, London: Routledge.

Morley, David and Roger Silverstone (1990), 'Domestic Communication –

Technologies and Meanings', *Media, Culture and Society*, Vol. 12, No. 1, pp. 31–55.

Moyal, Ann (1989), 'The Feminine Culture of the Telephone: People, Patterns and Policy', *Prometheus*, Vol. 7, No. 1, pp. 5–31.

Mulgan, Geoff (ed.) (1990), *The Question of Quality*, London: British Film Institute.

Murdock, Graham (1993), 'Communications and the Constitution of Modernity', *Media, Culture and Society*, Vol. 15, No. 4, pp. 521–39.

Ochberg, Richard (1994), 'Life Stories and Storied Lives', in Amia Lieblich and Ruthellen Josselson (eds), *The Narrative Study of Lives: Exploring Identity and Gender*, Thousand Oaks: Sage, pp. 113–44.

Olwig, Karen Fog and Kirsten Hastrup (eds) (1997), *Siting Culture: The Shifting Anthropological Object*, London: Routledge.

O'Sullivan, Tim (1991), 'Television Memories and Cultures of Viewing, 1950–65', in John Corner (ed.), *Popular Television in Britain: Studies in Cultural History*, London: British Film Institute, pp. 159–81.

Pahl, Jan (1990), 'Household Spending, Personal Spending and the Control of Money in Marriage', *Sociology*, Vol. 24, No. 1, pp. 119–38.

Pecheux, Michel (1982), *Language, Semantics and Ideology: Stating the Obvious*, Basingstoke: Macmillan.

Pegg, Mark (1983), *Broadcasting and Society 1918–39*, London: Croom Helm.

Petrie, Duncan and Janet Willis (eds) (1995), *Television and the Household: Reports from the BFI's Audience Tracking Study*, London: British Film Institute.

Punter, David (1986), 'The Unconscious and Contemporary Culture', in David Punter (ed.), *Introduction to Contemporary Cultural Studies*, Harlow: Longman, pp. 252–74.

Radway, Janice (1987), *Reading the Romance: Women, Patriarchy and Popular Literature*, London: Verso.

Radway, Janice (1988), 'Reception Study: Ethnography and the Problems of Dispersed Audiences and Nomadic Subjects', *Cultural Studies*, Vol. 2, No. 3, pp. 359–76.

Rakow, Lana (1992), *Gender on the Line: Women, the Telephone and Community Life*, Urbana: University of Illinois Press.

Rampton, Ben (1995), *Crossing: Language and Ethnicity Among Adolescents*, Harlow: Longman.

Rath, Claus-Dieter (1985), 'The Invisible Network: Television as an Institution in Everyday Life', in Phillip Drummond and Richard Paterson (eds), *Television in Transition: Papers from the First International Television Studies Conference*, London: British Film Institute, pp. 199–204.

Reid, Elizabeth (1995), 'Virtual Worlds: Culture and Imagination', in Steven Jones (ed.), *CyberSociety: Computer-Mediated Communication and Community*, Thousand Oaks: Sage, pp. 164–83.

Robins, Kevin (1989), 'Reimagined Communities? European Image Spaces, Beyond Fordism', *Cultural Studies*, Vol. 3, No. 2, pp. 145–65.

Robins, Kevin (1991), 'Tradition and Translation: National Culture in Its Global Context', in John Corner and Sylvia Harvey (eds), *Enterprise and Heritage: Crosscurrents of National Culture*, London: Routledge, pp. 21–44.

Robins, Kevin (1996), 'Cyberspace and the World We Live In', in Jon Dovey (ed.), *Fractal Dreams: New Media in Social Context*, London: Lawrence and Wishart, pp. 1–30.

Rowntree, Seebohm (1941), *Poverty and Progress: A Second Social Survey of York*, London: Longman.

Said, Edward (1978), *Orientalism*, London: Routledge and Kegan Paul.

Scannell, Paddy (1988), 'Radio Times: The Temporal Arrangements of Broadcasting in the Modern World', in Phillip Drummond and Richard Paterson (eds), *Television and Its Audience: International Research Perspectives*, London: British Film Institute, pp. 15–31.

Scannell, Paddy (1989), 'Public Service Broadcasting and Modern Public Life', *Media, Culture and Society*, Vol. 11, No. 2, pp. 135–66.

Scannell, Paddy (ed.) (1991a), *Broadcast Talk*, London: Sage.

Scannell, Paddy (1991b), 'Introduction: The Relevance of Talk', in Paddy Scannell (ed.), *Broadcast Talk*, London: Sage, pp. 1–13.

Scannell, Paddy (1996), *Radio, Television and Modern Life: A Phenomenological Approach*, Oxford: Blackwell.

Scannell, Paddy and David Cardiff (1982), 'Serving the Nation: Public Service Broadcasting Before the War', in Bernard Waites, Tony Bennett and Graham Martin (eds), *Popular Culture: Past and Present*, London: Croom Helm, pp. 161–88.

Scannell, Paddy and David Cardiff (1991), *A Social History of British Broadcasting: Vol. 1, 1922–1939: Serving the Nation*, Oxford: Blackwell.

Schlesinger, Philip (1987), *Putting 'Reality' Together: BBC News*, London: Methuen.

Schlesinger, Philip (1991), *Media, State and Nation: Political Violence and Collective Identities*, London: Sage.

Sharma, Sanjay, John Hutnyk and Ashwani Sharma (eds) (1996), *Dis-Orienting Rhythms: The Politics of the New Asian Dance Music*, London: Zed Books.

Silverstone, Roger (1990), 'Television and Everyday Life: Towards an Anthropology of the Television Audience', in Marjorie Ferguson (ed.), *Public Communication – The New Imperatives: Future Directions for Media Research*, London: Sage, pp. 173–89.

Silverstone, Roger (1994), *Television and Everyday Life*, London: Routledge.

Silverstone, Roger, Eric Hirsch and David Morley (1991), 'Listening to a Long Conversation: An Ethnographic Approach to the Study of Information and Communication Technologies in the Home', *Cultural Studies*, Vol. 5, No. 2, pp. 204–27.

Silverstone, Roger, Eric Hirsch and David Morley (1992), 'Information and Communication Technologies and the Moral Economy of the Household', in Roger Silverstone and Eric Hirsch (eds), *Consuming Technologies: Media and Information in Domestic Spaces*, London: Routledge, pp. 15–31.

Silverstone, Roger and David Morley (1990), 'Families and Their Technologies: Two Ethnographic Portraits', in Tim Putnam and Charles Newton (eds), *Household Choices*, London: Futures Publications, pp. 74–83.

Slack, Jennifer Daryl (1989), 'Contextualising Technology', in Brenda Dervin, Lawrence Grossberg, Barbara O'Keefe and Ellen Wartella (eds), *Rethinking Communication: Vol. 2, Paradigm Exemplars*, Newbury Park: Sage, pp. 329–45.

Smith, Marc and Peter Kollock (eds) (1999), *Communities in Cyberspace*, London: Routledge.

Smythe, Dallas (1981), *Dependency Road: Communications, Capitalism, Consciousness and Canada*, Norwood: Ablex.

Sreberny-Mohammadi, Annabelle (1996), 'The Global and the Local in International Communications', in James Curran and Michael Gurevitch (eds), *Mass Media and Society*, 2nd edn, London: Arnold, pp. 177–203.

Thompson, Edward (1967), 'Time, Work-Discipline and Industrial Capitalism', *Past and Present*, No. 38, pp. 56–97.

Thompson, John (1988), 'Mass Communication and Modern Culture: Contribution to a Critical Theory of Ideology', *Sociology*, Vol. 22, No. 3, pp. 359–83.

Thompson, John (1990), *Ideology and Modern Culture: Critical Social Theory in the Era of Mass Communication*, Cambridge: Polity Press.

Thompson, John (1994), 'Social Theory and the Media', in David Crowley and David Mitchell (eds), *Communication Theory Today*, Cambridge: Polity Press, pp. 27–49.

Thompson, John (1995), *The Media and Modernity: A Social Theory of the Media*, Cambridge: Polity Press.

Thompson, Paul (1978), *The Voice of the Past: Oral History*, Oxford: Oxford University Press.

Tolson, Andrew (1991), 'Televised Chat and the Synthetic Personality', in Paddy Scannell (ed.), *Broadcast Talk*, London: Sage, pp. 178–200.

Tomlinson, John (1991), *Cultural Imperialism: A Critical Introduction*, London: Pinter.

Tomlinson, John (1999), *Globalisation and Culture*, Cambridge: Polity Press.

Turkle, Sherry (1988), 'Computational Reticence: Why Women Fear the Intimate Machine', in Cheris Kramerae (ed.), *Technology and Women's Voices*, New York: Routledge, pp. 41–61.

Turkle, Sherry (1996), *Life on the Screen: Identity in the Age of the Internet*, London: Weidenfeld and Nicolson.

Turner, Graeme (1990), *British Cultural Studies: An Introduction*, Boston: Unwin Hyman.

Urry, John (1990), *The Tourist Gaze: Leisure and Travel in Contemporary Societies*, London: Sage.

Urry, John (1991), 'Time and Space in Giddens' Social Theory', in Christopher Bryant and David Jary (eds), *Giddens' Theory of Structuration: A Critical Appreciation*, London: Routledge, pp. 160–75.

Volosinov, Valentin (1973), *Marxism and the Philosophy of Language*, New York: Seminar Press.

Wark, McKenzie (1994), *Virtual Geography: Living with Global Media Events*, Bloomington: Indiana University Press.

Werbner, Pnina (1988), 'Taking and Giving: Working Women and Female Bonds in a Pakistani Immigrant Neighbourhood', in Sallie Westwood and Parminder Bhachu (eds), *Enterprising Women: Ethnicity, Economy and Gender Relations*, London: Routledge, pp. 177–202.

Werbner, Pnina (1996), 'Funspaces: On Identity and Social Empowerment Among British Pakistanis', *Theory, Culture and Society*, Vol. 13, No. 4, pp. 53–79.

Williams, Raymond (1974), *Television: Technology and Cultural Form*, London: Fontana.

Williams, Raymond (1989), *Resources of Hope: Culture, Democracy, Socialism*, London: Verso.

Willis, Paul (1990), *Common Culture: Symbolic Work at Play in the Everyday Cultures of the Young*, Milton Keynes: Open University Press.

Wilson, Tony (1993), *Watching Television: Hermeneutics, Reception and Popular Culture*, Cambridge: Polity Press.

Wynne, Derek (1990), 'Leisure, Lifestyle and the Construction of Social Position', *Leisure Studies*, Vol. 9, No. 1, pp. 21–34.

Young, Filson (1933), *Shall I Listen? Studies in the Adventure and Technique of Broadcasting*, London: Constable.

# Index

163

Burgess, Jacquelin, 100

Cambridge, 48, 56, 61, 64, 109
Canadian, 81–2, 101, 124
capturing time and space in the home,
    1, 42–3, 47, 52
Cardiff, David, 44, 51, 55–6, 140–1
Carey, James, 104
*Casualty*, 77, 90, 92
Centre for Contemporary Cultural
    Studies, 99
Chaney, David, 23
Channel 4, 138
channel-hopping, 65–6
Charles, Nickie, 35–6
Chernobyl, 111
Children's Channel, 74
*Children's Hour*, 51
*Choosing the Right Food*, 52
Christmas, 55–6, 69, 89, 141
civil inattention, 108, 112, 114, 145
Clifford, James, 102, 117
CNN, 77, 80–1
code switching, 133
collapsing of space and time, 100
Collins, Richard, 98
communicative ethos of broadcasting,
    19–20, 22, 97
communicative unease, 19
communities in cyberspace, 141, 144–5
compulsion of proximity, 37, 145
computational reticence, 84
computer talk, 148
conservation, 61, 67, 71, 147
Conservative administration, 58
convergence, 136, 148–9
conversationalisation of public
    discourse, 22, 97
Corner, John, 16
*Coronation Street*, 140
cosy companionship of radio, 49–50
*Crossroads*, 29–30
*Crosswits*, 79
cultural circuit, 12–13
cultural economy, 30, 85, 90
culturalist perspective, 63
*Cyberia*, 148
cyclical time, 54

*Dallas*, 30–1
Dando, Jill, 113
decoding, 9, 16, 27–9, 33
defeminisation, 32
delivering audiences to advertisers, 23
democratisation of institutional talk, 98
deregulation, 3, 40, 57
*Desert Island Discs*, 140
diaspora space, 8
differential interpretations, 16, 28
disembedding, 6, 37, 39, 106–7,
    109–11
dish-erectors, 61, 147
disidentifications, 85, 98
distance from necessity, 86
distinction, 4, 16, 29–30, 57, 64–5, 90,
    124, 128–9
domestication, 5, 42, 52
domesticity, 19, 22, 50
*Donahue*, 23
Donzelot, Jacques, 95
double consciousness, 120
*Duchess of Duke Street*, 79

*EastEnders*, 32, 122, 140
Edinburgh, 8, 117, 120, 123–5, 127–9,
    131, 133, 147
Edwardian, 60, 67–8
electronic landscapes, 4, 39–41, 141
Ellis, John, 14–15, 19, 97
emergence of the family audience, 42,
    50
emotional labour, 108, 142
emotionally significant interaction, 30
emotional realism, 31
emptying of space, 106
English, 59–60, 89, 104, 133
entourage of technical goods, 62
*Eroticomm*, 142
*Esther*, 22
estrangement, 6, 15, 108–9, 136
European, 4, 40, 59, 65–6, 80, 94, 98,
    111
Eurosport, 69
expert systems, 37, 107–8, 111–12
explosion of discourse, 52
extended availability of symbolic
    forms, 8, 16, 26

synthetic personalisation, 22, 112

tabloid television, 59
Talk Radio, 138
taste warfare, 75, 147
technological determinism, 5, 96, 98, 101
*Teenage Mutant Hero Turtles*, 67
teleconferencing, 141
television without frontiers thesis, 98
televisual tourism, 65–6
territories of transmission, 4, 36, 41, 64, 132
The Beatles, 82
*The Big Breakfast*, 138
*The CyberCafé*, 148
*The Hot Line*, 143
*The Oprah Winfrey Show*, 23
theory of structuration, 5, 105
*The People's Food*, 54
*The Simpsons*, 62
*The Steve Allen Show*, 21
*The X Files*, 133
thick descriptions, 10
*This Morning*, 21–2
Thompson, Edward, 54
Thompson, John, 6, 8, 16–18, 26, 38, 109, 137–8
Thompson, Paul, 42
time-geography, 102–3
time-space compression, 100, 115, 119
time-space distanciation, 4–7, 106, 109–11, 119
*Top Gear*, 133
tourist gaze, 79
tragic structure of feeling, 31–2
transformation of interaction, 109

translation, 7–8, 117–18, 120, 125, 128, 132
transnational connections, 119
travelling cultures, 102
trust, 6, 107–8, 111–12, 115
Turkle, Sherry, 84, 143–4
TV reception as a routine social event, 33

UK Gold, 79
United States, 19, 23, 25, 33, 70, 79, 94, 112, 137, 142

*Vanessa*, 22
veridical effect, 110
virtual reality, 8, 143

Wark, MacKenzie, 104
Washington, Denzel, 128
*Watch with Mother*, 67
Welsh, 80–1
Werbner, Pnina, 127
Williams, Raymond, 4, 10, 13–14, 95–9
will to ordinariness, 21, 138
Wilson, Tony, 110
withdrawal to interior space, 5, 49, 95
*Wogan*, 22
Wohl, Richard, 9, 20–1, 112, 138
Women's International Day, 127
World Cup soccer, 110
*WWF Wrestling*, 77, 93
Wynne, Derek, 61

Young, Filson, 48, 55
*Your Zindgi*, 133

Zee, 132–3